<u>Jukebox Poets</u>

Townshend Cooper

This book is dedicated to the reader.

"When you don't know what you're living for, you don't care how you live from one day to the next. You're happy the day has passed and the night has come, and in your sleep you bury the tedious question of what you lived for that day and what you're going to live for tomorrow." – Ivan Goncharov, *Oblamov*

"Once well underground," he said, "you know exactly where you are. Nothing can happen to you, and nothing can get at you. You're entirely your own master, and you don't have to consult anybody or mind what they say. Things go on all the same overhead, and you let 'em, and don't bother about 'em. When you want to, up you go, and there the things are, waiting for you."- Kenneth Grahame, *The Wind in the Willows*

<u>Chapter 1</u>

Rarely have I felt as depressed as on the day that I was released from prison.

My life, once again, was forced to change routine, and this time I had absolutely no direction. Though I had been jailed for three months for committing no crime other than speaking, I had enjoyed the comfort of the concrete walls, the regular meals, the guarantee of solace and the hope of not being bothered by people. I had gotten used to it. Outside, I worried that I would once again find myself the center of unwanted attention.

"Maybe try to make some new friends when you're out, huh?" The guard had suggested, half-mockingly, half-serious, as I received back what little I had on me when I was arrested. He had pitied me, like a lot of the guards seemed to, and often joked and tried to make light of my circumstances in a way that was meant to be friendly but came off as self-serving. The clothes he brought to me were the same ones that I had been in on that night, and still smelled faintly of smoke and fire: a dark-blue hoodie and khakis, dirty and which were, unbeknownst to me at the time, now considered holy relics to some. I would've thrown them out then and there, but it was all that I had.

The torture of prison is the promise of rumination, or at least it must be for those guilty of the crimes of which they are convicted. My conscious was clear and my term was short, so in reality my months locked away were simply spent hoping that the long days would result in my name being forgotten by the time I got out. The routine of life on the inside soon became meditative, with hours comfortably fitting into slots of time for meals, reading, and exercise. My situation was particularly unique in that my reason for arrest was being played on television semi-regularly for a few days after my arrival, which made me worry that I would be accosted by someone looking to make some name for themselves. This wasn't a high-security facility by any means, and I didn't think I was in prison with anyone particularly violent, but you could never really tell, could you?

On my third day inside, an older, larger man must have seen that I was acting skittish because he saddled up next to me during breakfast. Without looking at me, he told me that as long as I kept my nose clean and didn't get in anyone's way, people who were inside for as short as I was weren't likely to face any real trouble.

I took the opportunity to ask the obvious. "Even if you were on TV?"

He turned and looked at me with total surprise, a flabby double chin of gray stubble and steel-cut oatmeal flapping ajar.

"You were on TV?" After that I never bothered speaking to anyone else and had no real problems.

"*Aah*, well," the guard slapped me on the back abruptly, shaking me awake and guiding me along. "Don't worry too much about it. You're out of here, at least." He was stocky and had a long red beard, and was escorting out myself and another, more prolific inmate to the front gate; someone who'd been in jail for roughly as long as I had, but who had engendered some level of respect among the general population. The guard had worked here for a long time, but was only a few years older than I was. "Everyone that comes out of here eventually finds their place."

I wasn't convinced. "You so sure about that?"

He chuckled but didn't say anything, the surface-level self-indulgent optimism dying on the spot. What on my entrance I remembered to be a long pathway from the prison center to the gates seemed to shrink now on my reluctant departure. On both sides of us were tall chain-linked fences, where some inmates had come to either pay their respects to the other prisoner departing, or to jeer at me.

"Try not to get anyone killed this time on the outside, huh kid?"

"You'll be back in here soon enough. Your types always are."

"You know what happens if you come here again? They put you in a *real* ward, with *real* criminals."

I ignored it. When I'd first arrived I was given some distance, because just to what extent I'd been involved with the crimes I was convicted of wasn't well known. As things became a little clearer, and as time moved on, the other prisoners had gotten bolder and started mocking - maybe in some perverse way jealous of all of the attention I had gotten.

But it was as if the guard hadn't heard a single word thrown at me. "I'm sure people have forgotten all about that stuff, kid," he said, giving me an awkward, half-hearted and much lighter pat on the back.

And with that, the steel doors closed behind me, severing our worlds with a bang. Now me and the other inmate were on the outside, under the shade of the huge, gray, barbed-wire adorned walls, waiting in silence on a dirt road that faced directly across into a ditch and the beginning of some sparse undeveloped field. Far away you could see the shadows of cars drifting slowly along the highway, but there was no sound save for the wind and muffled, faraway voices behind us.

The other guy was some greasy mobster type who had, by some connections, managed to have prepared for him a tailored, ironed pinstripe suit ready for his release. He was older, in his sixties, and handled himself with a casualness that indicated that he was not a stranger to prison and he would not be surprised if he had to return someday, like it was a vacation home or a timeshare he was obligated to come back to time and again.

He turned to finally acknowledge me and looked me up and down, trying to place my face. "So you're the famous one, huh?"

"I don't know about that."

"You were on the news a while back though, right?"

"Yeah."

"Don't worry, I won't ask. None of my business."

"I appreciate it."

He eyed me again. "You need work, kid?"

"Oh, no, no." I awkwardly stumbled over my words. "I'll be fine. Thank you, though." He shrugged.

"Here's my card, just in case." He flipped one out of his coat pocket and handed it to me. Something about *Quality Vacuum services* with a phone number and an address I never planned to find.

I was rooted awkwardly on the platform just outside of jail, dreading the future and trying to forget the past. And as I stood at the gate to where I had been so blissfully incarcerated, a spring breeze arose from the underbrush across the dirt road and swept towards me – trailing with it the stinging scent of wildflowers and of rain-soaked grass. Scents I had missed inside more than I thought I would, sensations bringing back vague memories of instances so long passed that their recollection and the feelings they engendered were much as brief as the breeze that summoned them. Yet this summoned no appreciation, no enjoyment or reevaluation of my status, and freedom felt burdened unto me as an unwanted responsibility.

The bus eventually arrived, and we were the only two people on it. It was a long silver one, the kind that you'd see in movies from the fifties that always looked like they'd be hell to ride in if they were under direct sunlight. Sure enough, the thing had no air conditioning. The mobster sat towards the front after slapping the driver's shoulder in an all-too-familiar manner, and I placed myself near the back and prepared for the long drive back into town. Despite trying to keep my mind off it, my thoughts naturally wandered to the past few months and how I ended up in this situation - with no job, no money, and apparently no future. It was all I had thought about and I never reached any sensible conclusion.

Most confusing was why I had been put in jail in the first place. I had no idea. Even to this day, after so much has happened, I still feel it to be a gross miscarriage of justice that I had ever seen the inside of a prison cell, and yet I appeared alone in my incredulity, or at least I did not grasp the full extent of my responsibility. I had been a student at university, and, after being approached by a pair of individuals, I was in short exploited for my lifestyle and my views by their radical friends. To the eyes of most my existence was alarmingly tame, but to them, this same lassitude was treated as inspirational. And this was used to their advantage, though I either didn't care, or didn't notice, or, more likely, didn't understand or even pay attention. Only after things fell apart (or went according to plan, depending on who you asked) did I realize that my role was much larger than being simply the aloof onlooker I thought I was.

From what I understood, this mentality that was projected onto me appealed to a majority of the student body as a whole. Before I could grasp the full gravity of what it was that the people around me were trying to accomplish, everything came to a head in what came to be called the "High Street Riots". Three people were killed, hundreds were injured and eight buildings were set on fire. Following a speech my compatriots forced me to give – atop an apartment complex on the main street, where the rioters gathered below us – the university campus was overrun by students. The police quelled the rioting, eventually, and I was hauled away to one of the precincts. My words, which ironically I played no part in writing, set spark to the already incensed masses, and they found reason within to begin a pointless revolt, one of which the leaders must have hoped would spread.

If it is not already obvious, let me be clear, to anyone who remembers or who was there: I had no such desires. All I wanted to do was go back to my little apartment off campus and sleep.

I could understand why I had been arrested along with everybody else initially, but I was shocked when I was told that I was being charged with inciting a riot. Every individual that had participated in the events pointed to me as being the catalyst for their temporary insanity, an excuse and a scapegoat for them to blame instead of alcohol and personal irresponsibility. Myself and a few others spent actual time incarcerated. Everybody else, who wasn't convicted of assault, or murder, or arson, and was anonymous in the crowd, went back to their lives as students, pleased that they had gotten away with some rambunctious college fun – simply building memories for them to look back fondly upon while I quietly became acquainted with the walls of a cell and tried to ponder how I had ended up there. I was relieved that nothing but a spring breeze greeted me at the gate when I left. All clambering to be a martyr. All a rebellious, artistic soul. I was forgotten, or so I hoped.

At this point in my reminiscing I looked over at the mobster and was suddenly annoyed by his hand movements for a reason I could not place. He was rubbing the thumb of his right hand individually over each of the nails of the same hand in a manner that struck me as overly confident, overly self-assured. It was the subtle sensuality of the movements and the absent-mindedness by which he did it that bothered me. He was saying that he's a big shot. That he wears a nice suit and a nice watch. He knows you're looking at him and he's playing along like he doesn't. All I could do was look away and back out the window.

Eventually we arrived downtown. It was late at night by this point, and I had fallen asleep. We must've passed a stop already, because the mobster had gotten off. As I stood up to get off at the second stop, something fell off of my lap - he had dropped two $100 bills on me as I was sleeping. Charity out of pity maybe, but it was an act of generosity which at that point in time was invaluable, and for which I was deeply grateful, and which made me feel embarrassed that I'd gotten so annoyed for something so innocuous earlier.

This gift allowed me to purchase lodging at the hostel where I was headed for longer than I originally had the funds for. My only knowledge of hostels as a place of lodging came from colleagues who had backpacked through Europe on journeys of self-discovery naturally paid for by someone else, where they were romanticized if women were talking about them as a meeting place for like-minded travelers, or described as near-brothels and sites of ludicrous sexual conquest if it was a man bringing them up.

It wasn't in the best part of town, but it was located far away from my old campus and was cheap enough that I should have had enough time to find a job before I ran out of money. Hidden away behind a department store it stood, run down, with yellow paint chipped off of the outside walls and the sign advertising its name faded away with age and neglect. Inside was no better. The carpet was stained and torn up where it met the walls, whose wallpaper was yellowing and peeling off. It stank of dust and mold, and the only light source was a chandelier with several fizzled out lightbulbs, and what light there was illuminated drifting clouds of filth. I was optimistic that I wouldn't run into anyone who would recognize me over here, but instantly all of my hopes of anonymity were unceremoniously shattered as soon as I saw the front desk attendant's eyes light up as I checked in.

"Get outta *town*," he guffawed. He was young, lanky, loud and smelled of skunky beer. "We got a local celebrity lodging here now, huh? Fall on hard times there, Che Guevara?"

I felt myself blushing with indignation and embarrassment. But thankfully it was late enough that no one else was around. I placed the cash for one night's stay on the counter. "Room for one, please."

However, he was not finished. "Your ass must have *just* gotten out. Serves you right for what you was doin'. You know my cousin goes to school here and he knows one of them folks who got hurt 'cause of your nonsense? You know that?"

"Room. For one, please."

He found a key but hadn't had his fill of shaming me. I guess this place needed the business badly if he wasn't going to turn me out then and there. "And what happened to that girl you palled around with? *Elizabeth*, yeah, that was her name," He was rummaging around now for some liability form in another drawer which was missing a handle and which creaked horribly when he opened and shut it. "That slut. The one that got around, you know. And that one other freak you people - "

At this point my glare must have been venomous, because when he turned to look back at me his laughter finally dissipated and he quietly placed the key on the counter. I signed the form and silently trudged upstairs and found my small closet of a room.

Of course I knew who he was referring to. There were only a few faces that I remembered from my time in university (I could never go back – that was out of the question), two of which who, in my opinion, incited those events, and left the blame to me. Elizabeth was one of them. She was credited with "discovering" me, the one who introduced me to others, and began my career as an unwilling figurehead. A drug-addled girl who was convinced of her own brilliance, she read aloud the poems of dead men and faked tears at empty words on paper, a constant figure at underground coffeeshops and a proud, notorious outcast of every poetry society you could name. Bukowski was her favorite. She would regularly admonish others for the smallest instances of disagreement, pick venomous fights over imagined insults, and as a result, she had few friends. On her left hand, reading from the tip of her thumb to the tip of her forefinger, and crossing the skin in-between, was a proclamation of her desperately desired beatnik roots, a slogan, in bold, reading **"Cigarettes Are Cool"**. She too was hauled away by the authorities. I think she was fairly disheveled by the night's events. Either that, or she was still on acid and thus incomprehensible.

Then there was the "freak", the person I was told to call Dead Richard. I can't really describe him in the terms I would a real person, because Dead Richard seemed more a figment of the imagination given a pulse and body who happened to exist in the shared collective consciousness. The best I can do is illustrate him physically. A man of average height, slim, wearing something resembling a blue suede tracksuit jacket with a collar that reached up his neck, jeans, sneakers, and a white bucket hat with a single brown stripe circling the brim. He wore dirty white gloves, the kind you'd see some butler or something wear, and was never seen without his mask which hid the entirety of his face - that of an otter, and his eyes were always covered by some black, see-through material. He did not speak one word, and he never deviated from this costume; no skin was visible underneath. Dead Richard was, and remains, a complete and total enigma. I could not declare with confidence his purpose or his measure of sanity. He was simply there, yet his presence alone commanded confusing awe that not even the planners of the riots could muster. He did not indulge in the same pleasures as Elizabeth did, those of wild sex and drug abuse. His resolve was shown to be solid, though he did not speak, and surprisingly he proved himself very capable when several fights broke out within which I was caught.

I believe he approved of me, in a way, though if I were meant to take this as a high honor, I didn't. Rumors spread among the fearful students who know of him said he was homeless, and indeed I came across him sleeping on park benches and in doorways on several occasions. More rumors circulated of what had happened to him after the riots began to quell down, the most pervasive one being that he had been discovered dead in an alleyway, having shot himself. For some reason I found myself wishing that this was not true – but he disappeared, and I heard nothing about him while in prison. Faded away into obscurity, a strange memory you could confuse with a dream, had he not been captured on television and embedded in the stark memory of others, one of which you might have awoken from in a sweat some night and tried to place some meaning to, but would find that no meaning existed. In a world of monikers and aliases, he clearly held a place separate from all else, largely, I think, due to the capriciousness of his costume, with a purpose or goal that no one could seem to pinpoint.

Both deserved their notoriety just as well as I did, if not more. I wondered briefly what had happened to them, but I decided it better to try and forget.

Laying in bed that night, listening to cockroaches scurry along the wooden floor underneath me, I evaluated my position once again. As it stood, I had no certain future. I was open to do what I wanted, to choose a path that most suited me: as days passed I sought odd jobs, tried to resettle, but I was still restless and irritated that all of this had happened, and at my situation. I was soon briefly employed as a gas station attendant, a janitor at the department store next door, and a landscaping laborer. But in every scenario, it didn't last long - either because my past would come up, or because I couldn't stand what I was doing.

Weeks after my release, the mourning of my misdirected prospects was interrupted by a call - my grandmother, a venerable woman living on the western coast near San Francisco, had heard one way or another of my recent return to the outside world and immediately, almost commandingly reached out and invited me to California.

"How dare you not tell me about any of this?" She bristled over the phone. Her usually cheery and quiet voice was the sharpest I had heard in a long time. "What have you been doing? Where are you?"

" I'm sorry. I'm in a hostel on the other side of town. It's...It's been rough. I would have reached out and told you sooner."

Her anger quickly subsided. "Come out here," She demanded. "We'll get you back on your feet just yet - this is all a setback, is all. You just have to get a new start."

I quickly swallowed my pride and self pity, using the last of my money to book a plane ticket the day she sent word of her offer. A few days later when I departed the front desk attendant, eyes sunken in his head with a hangover, eyed my bags and called out, scathingly,

"You can run all you like but there's no escaping your sins, boy." In a moment of rage I threw my room key with full force at him. He swore loudly and ducked, smacking his forehead on the desk as he did so.

I left that place behind and was on an eight hour plane ride across the barren mid-U.S., and soon beginning life anew amongst the cliff faces and romantic auburn twilight of Berkeley. Though originally apprehensive about the uncertainty of it all, I found this new town infinitely more appealing than where I was coming from in terms of aesthetics. My grandmother's small apartment above a grocery on Berkeley's main street became my new home, and for some reason, despite everything that had happened, I was pleased with the overall outcome. Things could have gone far worse for me, all things considered - and at least now I wasn't squatting in some dirty, roach-infested hostel. I could start over, genuinely this time.

<u>Chapter 2</u>

Adjusting was simpler than I had anticipated. Next door to the apartment was a small bookstore, and around ten minutes up the street was the Clermont hotel, of which my grandmother frequented often, and was a respected member. I was given free use of their tennis courts and pools, which kept me from becoming stagnant and wallowing in recollection of the past while I considered how to move forward. I decided not to seek an education at the collegiate level again – not because I feared denial of entry to one of Berkeley's private schools, but because I was discouraged by the experiences I had had previously in those environments. I would avoid academia altogether, if I could, and that would double for the students. For some reason the pupils in California seemed somehow even worse. Perhaps it was the money. The city stinks of it to newcomers, drifting like a giant miasma, and even after months of living there I was still not used to it.

I wasn't absent of the struggles that this choice implied. Without a college degree, finding a job proved to be nearly impossible, especially in the Bay area. My grandmother maintained that she was willing to take care of me as long as necessary, an offer for which I was truly appreciative, but which offended my pride. I wanted to become my own person as quickly as I could, though I knew this was not easily nor hurriedly accomplished. After several months of applications to dozens and dozens of openings in the smallest organizations and businesses, and having been turned down for each, I began to feel the incredible weight of my past and my decisions upon me like never before. A hopelessness washed over me as my existence became one that proved to only be a burden, and part of me wondered whether or not this was a numbness I could recuperate from. But Grandma was having none of it and not only did she admonish me for being so self-defeating, she joined me on my search.

One day, in her infinite patience and charity, she told me that she had found something. A small publisher had approached her and inquired about me - my actual name was mentioned – and they said that they wished to offer me an authoring position with their small, but evolving, publishing firm. My initial feelings of joy were almost instantly smothered by suspicion. I had not written much of anything important at college, or ever really, and that my name was mentioned implied that they had heard about me through certain channels, ones of which I was not aware of, but certain as to what they were connected to. The realization that this must have been related to those unmentionable events of my sophomore year struck me with fright: I had told no one of my plans to travel to California, and thus this search for me – by a group of people that I did not know existed, but who apparently had me in their focus – must have been on a colossal, frantic scale. That they had found me, these unknowns, was terrifying, and I originally emailed them (they'd given my grandmother their card) to find out why and how they'd pursued a college dropout.

She was fanning herself with the card as I carefully laid out my concerns to her. It was unreasonably hot in her apartment that day, not because of the weather, but because the AC was old. She finally grew exasperated with my worry.

"Oh, who gives a damn?" She snapped, "Will they pay you?"

An hour or so after I'd reached out to these people, my feelings changed on the matter, and I decided that it wasn't important why they'd chased me, or how I was discovered. The less I knew about them the better, and though I would hear their offer, I would be as separated from their organization as possible should I decide to accept it. I was getting desperate for money. Furthermore, previous experience had, if nothing else, proven that it was best to never be directly involved with a group whose convictions were too strongly held: those riots were proof of this, and I could only assume that these people were affiliated somewhat with those defeated rebels. I emailed them again with this new outlook.

They responded, very quickly, and obviously disappointed with my mindset. Whoever it was on the other end, though, was unsettlingly enthused to be speaking with me at all, even digitally, and they were ecstatic to hear that I was interested in the position – despite my laid-out terms of employment.

In short, the emissary explained that they represented an online journal, and that they were willing to pay me to write articles, opinionated ones, on subjects they gave to me which would be published under a pen name. These topics were to be rather general, dealing with ideas of morality. They didn't ask me to build up some sort of new philosophy or anything like that, but they seemed to have tapped into a market of people who would be interested in reading articles about these topics and figured that I would be someone who could make up something people would read based on what I had been through.

Frankly the idea of writing about these topics made me recoil - the idea of appealing to people who had been the rioters which put me in prison was maddening - but the amount they were offering was exceptional. I made it abundantly clear that not only was my identity to be kept a secret if I were to write for this "publication" (a term I thought they used *very* liberally), but that I was not planning on repeating the incidents that had garnered me this proposal in the first place. I would not be attributed another demonstration in my name, and my articles, whatever they were on, would reflect this. If by chance some maniac, thrashing in the whips of existential despair should for some reason accredit their late-night deviancy to something I'd written, the publisher, not the author, would take full blame, and I would immediately quit. This last demand especially thrilled my correspondent, it seemed, because although I made it clear that I was toning myself down considerably, that I felt the need to address the possibility of such an event not only made it a scenario with some validity, but I had finally addressed my past and my relation to it.

The deep irony that I hadn't actually written any of the things that these people were so fascinated with didn't escape me. My words were just words before I was made into this fraudulent symbol for...whatever it was I was supposed to be. It now felt, in a way, as if everything were spoken through someone else's mouth. The whole thing was surreal, and in honesty, I made no effort to come to terms with any of it in any meaningful way.

They agreed to everything, and I was given a hefty pay for everything I wrote. I began a week later, and my heart sunk slightly for what I'd agreed to, but the salary was very good for such menial work, and the emphasis I'd placed on confidentiality *almost* reassured me that I would be safe from any former disciples. But in reality, they were paying a fraud who knew the style they were looking for. Served them right.

It had been four months since I was released from prison. I had moved to a new city. I had gotten a well paying job. At this point, I was very pleased. I would write as many articles as needed in order to get a place of my own, preferably close by, as I enjoyed Berkeley, and from there, I could live peacefully. The prospect made me excited: everything would be as it should soon enough, with a life of my own choosing.

Unfortunately, although the journal did pay well, it was unavoidable that it would be some time before I could afford to strike out alone. California's high cost of living was not exaggerated, and my grandmother revealed to me that the only way she could afford her apartment was because she had lived there before prices skyrocketed. I had to continue to work and be patient, and eventually, it would pay off: there was a nice little one-bedroom affair near the water that I had my eye on, that was adjusted between San Francisco and my grandmother's neighborhood. It had a fantastic view of the ocean as it bled out into the Pacific, and thus it was even more expensive than most – but it would be worth it.

This high goal meant that I had to work for quite a while, and although I wrote articles a few times a week (the first one they asked me to write on was on my opinions on the integrity of some currently running politicians, whom I had not heard of, so I simply made something up), I found that I had a lot of free time. I continued to make use of the Clermont facilities, and I read often at the bookstore down the street, but eventually, these resources were tired, and I became slightly bored. I took up running in the early morning hours, exploring the old homes hidden away in the bayside neighborhood under the foliage of dozens of variants of trees, jogging through dense fog along thick, cracked slabs of cement uprooted by thick, aggressive roots, passing rotting wooden fences and majestic gardens fit for some aristocratic family not of this era. Berkeley is full of artists who are somehow incredibly rich, and every home reflected some quirk of their owner. Garish displays would thrust out from the sidings and some bigger pieces were on occasion displayed proudly on the front lawn.

It was on one of these excursions that I came across an unusual sight. As time went on and my routes became more and more elaborate and encompassing the Berkeley jungle, one morning I passed a large, baby-blue, rusted Ford pickup in someone's front lawn. A cardboard sign read "For Sale - $3500" against the filthy windshield.

I am by no means a car aficionado nor a fanatic about vehicles in particular, though I'd had some acquaintances who were enamored with the love for a strong machine. I can appreciate aesthetic beauty, however, on the most plebeian level, and when I looked at this relic – it must have been a product of the seventies – I was drawn to the ruggedness. I decided I had made good headway on my goal for the apartment, and I needed a way to get around aside from walking (or so I assumed I would, to pursue future prospects), so to expand my horizons and allow for greater exploration, I purchased the heavily out-of-shape behemoth a day or so later, from a man with dark, heavy eyes and a hygiene akin to the state of the car he was selling. The pickup was bombastically loud for the first few weeks that I drove it. I'm certain that a few neighbors no doubt threw poisonous glances in my direction whenever I decided to take it out, but the thunderous motor was soon quieted after a quick, if costly, visit to a nearby mechanic, who, so in love with the machine, gave me a discount just because he considered it a joy to work on.

<u>Chapter 3</u>

The first thing that I did, when my car was considered ready, was traverse the highways of California for several hours until I reached a beach in Santa Cruz. I spent the whole day there, watching the waves swell high and listening to the distant uproar of a pier filled with rides. Sprawled on the white sand and dozing off as the sun set over a blinding horizon aflame with pink and orange clouds, the crowds dispersed, and a few bonfires spawned up from the dunes around me.

Feeling unusually precarious, perhaps because of the blissful day of sunbathing, or the renewed sense of endeavor I had found in my freedom, I jumped up and approached one such gathering. The young adults gathered wore sandals and donned dreadlocks, but they were universally accommodating towards all strangers, and made room for me around their pyre of driftwood. They offered me a beer after asking my name, though I declined the beer and gave them a fake identity.

They asked me where I was from and what I was doing, all of which I answered with a lie. As pleasant as their company may have been, the threat of recognition always lingered in my mind. The gathering went on late into the evening, with some grabbing wakeboards and diving into the water, some laughing and telling stories, some smoking, and everyone, at some point, very drunk.

Sometime in the early morning, as everyone began to lay out and sleep – or walk home, if they were fortunate enough to live close enough to such a place – one slapped me on the shoulder, startlingly, and slurred his name to me: Thomas.

Thomas, dressed in a t-shirt advertising "The Who" and still wearing sunglasses, proceeded to tell me how much he respected me and how great it was that he and I were now friends. Having had experience with the heavily intoxicated, I thanked him and agreed, knowing that we would never see each other again. Then, suddenly solemn, he told me a story, one which took me by surprise in its sudden earnesty.

When he was eight years old, Thomas, living in Indiana, was playing with some cousins one day. His family was fairly well-off, and they had acres and acres of woodland behind their home, the hub of he and his cousin's many adventures. On this particular day, Thomas, jumping over a creek, slipped and landed awkwardly on some rocks, breaking his ankle. His mother came for him, deep in this forest, and carried him back inside, trudging through mud and leaves in a bright yellow sundress, and nurtured him back to health for weeks as he recovered. He told me that this memory brings him to the brink of bitter tears – because he knows that one day, that woman will be gone.

I was aware of the loosened tongue that often accompanied alcohol, and such confessions were not entirely new to me. I had been the victim of a few back at school.Thomas finished his as the sun crept up behind us, and indeed, he seemed to be on the verge of genuine tears as I decided it was time for my departure. I thanked him – sincerely – and told him we would meet again. But he looked up at me as I stood, as if I had never been there, then glanced embarrassed to the sands, maybe coming off of his drunken stupor just enough to realize the emotional confession he had admitted to a complete stranger. I considered whether it was viable for me to ever return to Santa Cruz as I walked towards the dark carnival rides, whose light bulbs glowed in the rays of the rising sun. I soon came to the conclusion that everyone must, at some point or another, encounters such oddities when dealing with other people, and thus my experience was no different than another person's. I could return to the beach and have no unhealthy memories save that I knew one of the most hidden corners of a stranger's heart, which was, after all, no different than anyone else's. I was pleased that this place was not spoilt for me, though I reprimanded myself on the drive back to San Francisco for casually strolling into what could have been a dangerous situation, but settled with the excuse that the alcohol served as enough of a safeguard from recognition. I was due another article online, and I decided to write about the previous evening, while of course changing around names to disguise all of those involved.

The next few weeks were uneventful, but lounging about in Berkeley is pleasant in itself. Waking up to watch the mist seep through cobblestone roads under an orange sunrise, with the smell of coffee coming from the other room – and falling asleep as lamplights begin to glow in the darkness, as couples take to the streets, huddled side by side as warm rain spills into pools on the pavement. It was during this time, however, that I had a short period of recurring nightmares. Each evening would be the same, and it was only after I had dreamt the same thing several times that I recognized its origin, and that this was not so much a bad dream, but a suppressed memory from the riots - awakened by what exactly, I couldn't say.

It was the same night during which I was carried off to jail. This had happened during the preliminary stages of the whole affair, when things were still mostly quiet but there was a growing tension in the air. At around 7:30 p.m. I was walking into a dingy, filthy hookah bar – whose name I won't print, and has since been torn down, from what I understand. It was billed as a quote-unquote "base of operations" for those most closely associated with the evening riots, though I couldn't make such an assumption myself, as it was almost always packed with all sorts of people, loud, and stinking of flavored smoke.

However, the night of the riots, the place was completely empty. I had gone there with Elizabeth, for no other reason than I felt that something large was happening, and that this may have likely been the epicenter. Things had already started somewhere downtown, and word was that the people behind it were the people we knew.

The door was completely ajar, and as we stepped inside, Elizabeth was called into the other room by some mindless degenerate who had no relation at all with the events of the night or the movement that spurred them, aside from the holy fact that he supplied many of its members with drugs. He and Elizabeth enjoyed a casual relationship, and, in typical fashion, she abandoned me to lose herself behind some silken curtains.

I was left on my own. Though the place had always been dirty, it seemed today as if an earthquake had manifested directly beneath its foundations, and torn everything asunder. Behind the bar immediately in front of the entryway, bottles of alcohol lay shattered and seeping into the rotted carpet – chairs overturned: in the other room, old couches had their stuffing ripped out of them, large, beautifully intricate pipes smashed upon the ground, tables broken or flipped. In the corner, another vagrant slept, a woman I did not recognize, a bottle of wine next to her.

I climbed the spiral staircase into the basement, each step echoing on the metal bars as I descended. The building, before turning into such a hovel, had the history of being a bakery or something along those lines, and curved brick walls which once held great furnaces sheltered enclaves of handed-down furniture, and this too was tossed about. Strewn on the concrete floor were hundreds of pamphlets advertising local music groups, book readings, poetry sessions and more. These all fluttered calmly under an old ceiling fan, now barely hanging by a few cords, and one of its blades missing. The soft off rhythm whirring was the only thing breaking the silence.

I called out the name of the owner, whose room was at the end of the basement. He lived here, a man a little older than Elizabeth and I, who, in our few conversations, tended to lean on topics a bit more radical. I called out his name again, to no answer, and went to open the door. Something blocked it. I put my shoulder into it the second time, and with some scraping of something behind, it swung open.

His room was intact, or at least no messier than the first few times I had seen it. His bunk bed, his desk, table, television, all untouched. I figured he had gone wherever the customers had fled to, until I turned to leave.

I did not recognize, at first, what it was that was tied around the doorknob, and leading down behind that black head to end in a knot around his neck. It was a belt – his belt, as his loose pants, soiled and sticking to the floor around his waist implied. He leaned against the door, arms loosely at his sides, eyes bloodshot and rolled up – and tongue poking out of his mouth. He had taken his own life, but for what reason exactly, I never learned.

I quickly retreated from that place and met Elizabeth upstairs, who was clearly already on something. She lolled out a question to whether or not I had found the owner, to which I replied that I did not.

This nightmare occurred for six or seven days, and left me sleep-deprived and agitated. In an attempt to counteract this, I began to drive around late at night, to stave off sleep and the uncomfortable memories that it brought. I would sleep only a little when I returned home, but it would be uninterrupted, and I would be at peace. I drove along highways, backstreets, with only the faded orange glow of streetlights to keep me awake: the torn seats of that beat-up antique alit moments at a time in dying light, then to return to darkness until I passed under another, until I drove further. I ended up passing a lot of things those nights – homeless sleeping on park benches and in bushes, drunken, young couples fighting, and myriads of students on the streets. It was one of those nights, as I drove along one of the lonelier, hidden freeways of southern San Francisco, that I passed by the mural. On the right of the highway was a towering, concrete-plaster wall running along the length of the road, separating the drivers from the sloping hillside that began at its top and bent upwards towards the east. I thought nothing of the great painting as I approached it, but as I drove past, I recognized several faces staring blankly at me from the stone, and my truck screeched to a loud, abrupt halt.

The mural depicted my home city in flames – golden and amber wisps of fire encroached and enveloped entire buildings, and several well-known monuments from that area. Little black shadow figures ran around the fires, throwing things, holding signs, fighting the police. Above the scene was written "Never Forget the High Street Riot" in bold black lettering, followed by the date of the riots, as well as the name of the city.

Floating on either side of the mural were faces, the ones I had known: That of Elizabeth, yellow locks and that impertinent, glaring smirk. Under her was written her silly "Cigarettes Are Cool" slogan. Dead Richard's masked face and white hat smiled from across the city. A few others, drawn in smaller stature and with less reverence, under these two. I recognized them all. Each a ghost, a sad memory, a martyr for a cause that never really even existed. It made me uncomfortable to see them again.

I should mention here that while Dead Richard was certainly the most notable, he was not the only outrageous individual that populated the college area at that time. There were a few others that commanded the attention of the apostles of those hazy, odd days: "Mr. 3:16", a mocking nickname given to a student who dressed as a priest and screamed gospel at the steps of the university library every afternoon; "B&E Betty", a girl who had made the local news for her string of burglaries, the profits of which she then donated to charity. These were a few. But while these local legends stirred up conversation, it was Dead Richard who was whispered of. Dead Richard, the homeless, masked boy, the fearful specter who dominated the consciousness of the so-called "movement's" inner circle. He was untouchable, unmatched in the influence that his ghastly persona shrugged off. But ultimately, the roles they played didn't matter, as everyone met a similar end.

I was relieved to see that I had not made it onto the gross shrine, until I looked back up at the words above the city and realized in horror that I had been painted above that. There I was, placed above all of the others - my expression, blank. Only no name was written under my bust. Regardless, the discovery shook me, and I resolved to fix this by buying several cans of white paint and erasing this offense from the hidden road it was perched on. I did this the following night. I thought no more of it, as I came across not similar memorials, and concluded that this must've been the work of one single, troubled individual.

Eventually my nightmares went away, but my nightly cruisings continued. I had taken a liking to steering aimlessly in the darkness or perhaps sought to stave off any other buried memories waiting to rear their ugly head, watching as I passed by the scenes and untold stories of the evenings. Back in the east, I rarely left my apartment following the conclusion of the day's activities – that is, prior to meeting Elizabeth – and the freedom that I was allowed here was enjoyable. The San Francisco bay between Berkeley and its imposing neighbor became my favorite spot to meander around. I watched the flow of the tide of and the traveling tail lights from cars, in the city, as the moon or the clouds were mirrored in a choppy fashion under the sky. It was peaceful. In the dead of night, you could park near the water for a minute, breathe in the smell of salt and sand and feel the weight finally start to slip from your shoulders.

In this particular part of the coast that I frequented, near the sandy tides was a small building, indistinguishable and alone. It was made of red brick, covered in algae, and the end of which faced the waters. I didn't realize this the first time I saw it, but the building had only one large window, looking across the water to San Francisco. There were always a few cars parked near it, but for all the times I'd driven near it or past it, I hadn't the slightest idea of what it was supposed to be. It looked almost solemn, at the end of the road where asphalt turns to sand, and finally I grew intrigued, and ventured to look closer.

I remember that night being particularly windy as I parked and walked around to the entrance. A small front door with an "open" sign appeared on a small wooden stairway on the northern end facing the beach, and next to the door, a black plaque which read, in white lettering, "bar". There was no name, no address. I entered, if for no other reason than to seek temporary shelter, a decision which ultimately I am not sure I regret or am thankful for.

How can I adequately describe the place which was to become my home, my unspoilt little corner of the world? It was dark: brown hazel panels on the floor and unmatched furniture mingled with exposed, choppy red brick on the walls. It was two storied, a spiral wooden staircase on my right leading up to the second floor. A long bar was on my left, the wall behind it lined with glowing cases of alcohol illuminated by golden light. Old couches and lounge chairs stood between tables with bar stools. The place was poorly lit, save for some wall lanterns, the underglow of the bar, and the dim moonlight streaming in from the massive, floor-to-ceiling window that took up the majority of the back wall. It seemed a cozy, intimate, albeit dusty and a little run down hideaway, and on this particular night it was sparse of patrons, perhaps three or four present.

I went up to the bar and ordered a beer from the girl behind it, and was enjoying myself until one of the customers stood up and approached the large window in the back, where I noticed a previously hidden jukebox of exquisite condition, clean of every imaginable smudge or crack or smear of grime that usually comes with a bar jukebox, almost like it was brand new. The customer walked up to it, put in a quarter, and the thing burst into light as it was brought alive. Gay neon emanated from the back corner of the bar as disks flipped, until a choice was settled upon, and the patron, satisfied with his selection, returned to his seat.

I was anticipating a song, of course, following those silent moments as the machine began to whirr and work, and was speechless when the record began playing.

A scratching voice rolled out from the speakers of this shining obelisk, and after a brief moment of disbelief did I realize that someone had began to recite something:

Midway upon the journey of our life
I found myself in a forest dark,
For the straightforward pathway had been lost.

My immediate reaction, following the initial shock, was disgust. This mingled with confusion and wonderment, and, bewildered, I quickly paid for my beverage and departed, almost dizzily. Instantly I was reminded of the desperation for artistic merit that had so consumed Elizabeth and those she associated with back home, and stumbled back to my truck against the biting wind as memories of smokey poetry readings and bar fights plumed up in my head. But I fear that I know myself better than I give credit, for I knew, as I drove away, that that place had dug its claws into me, and I was captured.

A jukebox that played poetry, in a secluded bar by the beach – I have one great flaw, a flaw I can only suppress as much as I am able, a flaw that I can attribute to the riots to which I am accredited and to all major disasters in my life. I am drawn, inexplicably, and with a singular great, almost instinctual passion, towards the incredulous. People who fall outside of all categories, who exist and live with reckless, self-destructive and purposeless abandon. And though the memories of the riots still burned, fresh in my mind, serving as evidence against all associations with these types, I could not help myself. Such a place as that gave all indications as a hub for these people, a nest. Cursing myself for my weakness, I went to that bar regularly following that fateful night, to do naught but people watch and sate my appetite for the unpredictable. Thus truly began my life in Berkeley.

<u>Chapter 4</u>

I was able to hide myself away in a corner of the uppermost floor most days, blending in while I listened quietly to the people around me. I either sat there, or, if I wanted to change it up a bit and see how those who inhabited the lower levels lived their lives, I'd switch to another unremarkable spot below. Between upstairs and downstairs, nobody was safe from my eavesdropping, and I found myself listening in on some delicious conversations – the likes of which I had hoped to encounter in such a place, glimpses into the lives of the people who could stand a bar where the jukebox played poetry. I noticed pretty quickly that the place had a few regulars, people from the surrounding area who had one way or another stumbled here, and made it their ancestral home. In fact, it was almost made up exclusively of regulars.

There was an old man, a veteran of some war or another who had lost his legs while serving his country, who would, every Monday morning, roll in on his wheelchair – whose rusted, iron wheels had long lost their rubber coating, and now scraped horrendously along the wooden panels. His eyes were startlingly bright, and he had a short, gray, dirty beard which was almost always matted with sand. He was never without his dog tags and bandana both tied around his forehead, and on these weekly visits he always had with him a string of dried fish, which he would try to sell to the bartender, and when she wouldn't hear any of it, he would laugh it off, and buy something to drink. All the while he would casually bring up the quality of his "catch", and after a few more firm denials, he would get frustrated and roll out of the building, swearing silently to himself as he did. I believe his name was Eddie, and you could always tell when he had entered the building no matter where you sat because the scratching from his wheels and his dog tags tapping together traveled far.

Also present most of the time was a young man with short, curly hair and some thin blonde stubble who sat in the back of the main room openly reading pornography, pouring over it like it was some sort of scholarly text, while drinking a long-island iced tea. Books of smut and outrageous fetishes would be piled all around his little workstation as he read, deeply intrigued and fascinated, studying each work as if they were the most eye-opening and important pieces of literature ever written. Sometimes an older woman would come in, who had enormous horn-rimmed glasses and always wore several layers of thick, multi-colored fabric as a robe, no matter the weather. I assumed she was an art teacher, due to a heated conversation she had with the pornographic student. She had been furiously demanding that he put away such scandalous, rude material, and he had once retaliated that it was a form of art. She scoffed, telling him that "Well you wouldn't see that in *my* classroom". Regardless, the boy was unbothered and did not stop his routine, and the woman made it a point to snap at him at least several times whenever she and he were both in the building together. She had even appealed to the bartender to remove him, but she just waved her off, so she was resigned to sulk in some back corner somewhere with a glass of white wine while occasionally shaking her head in disgust.

On the second floor sat a young Asian girl, with black hair and very neatly trimmed bangs, who was constantly producing music on her computer. Every now and again she would take out her headphones to hear her latest creation on the speakers, which could've ranged from classical piano to a thick, vibrating sound you'd likely hear if you went to a either an electronica concert or a factory production line. As a result, her presence was either nearly unnoticeable or seriously jarring to the other patrons. The only times that she did not indulge in this practice of sharing her music aloud was when the jukebox was playing some poem – a tactic, I assumed, that was due to past experiences where her creations had interrupted the recording and annoyed other patrons.

There was also a young couple who would occupy her space nearby, sitting on one of the couches, mostly talking quietly to one another, or in some extreme cases, kissing rather passionately, an act which drew the ire of the producer who sat not too far from them. When this occurred for longer than was appropriate, she would nonchalantly pull out her headphones and play, for a few seconds and very loudly, one of her more startling tracks, shocking the pair out of their coalescence. Their names were Benjamin and Katie, and this was made public knowledge during my third month of visitation to the bar, where one busy night an enormous dispute exploded between the two of them, and they did not reappear for a week and a half. Finally, on the bottom floor there appeared every once and awhile a group of three young men, two thin, studious ones and one massive muscular one, who were often engaged in discussion ranging from politics, to weightlifting, to cartoons. Aside from these constants, there was on occasion a mish-mash of patrons who wandered into the bar, all of them almost always as interesting as I had hoped.

Naturally, the personalities of the usuals did not become known to me immediately, and I only gained a glimpse of them as my visits to the bar continued. I felt a little ashamed and embarrassed in the beginning, when I still had some feelings of paranoia or perhaps guilt about the whole situation, and only began to calm myself when I realized that nobody really paid attention to me. I was still paranoid, so much of the time I would walk in with a baseball cap on and my head either down or facing out the window, for fear of being recognized. I would spend a few hours a day at the bar, usually in the afternoon or perhaps stop by in the evening, and once or twice I would bring along my own articles to work on for their submission to my online employer. But in all honesty, in the earlier period, as my visits went on and on, I did not witness very much of the eccentricity of which I thought may have gathered here. Not much seemed to distinguish it from any other bar – I was unaware of the intricacies of the usual patrons, as I did not yet know them well enough – and I thought that perhaps my earlier assessment had been off.

This doubt was wiped away one Wednesday towards the end of my first month of patronage, when I was sitting on the top floor, alone, listening to any conversation around me. Naturally a bar does not attract many customers during the midday in the midweek, but because there were less people present, I believed that this allowed me to better listen in on those who did come, as there was much less background noise or chatter, and the acoustics of the place allowed, for some reason, for noise to travel far in some spots. I was attempting to listen in on a couple downstairs, who were seated right below where I was, as they discussed what I could only make out to be the subject of illegal dog fighting, when a stranger appeared and sat across from me. So absorbed was I in trying to eavesdrop on the customers downstairs that I did not notice him until he cleared his throat, startling me.

He was a man of African heritage, with an intensely dark complexion. His pigmentation was so deep that it could have been compared to a rich velvet, but he had clear laugh lines around his mouth, and when he smiled, as he was doing now, creases appeared on the corners of his eyes, and it was as if his skin was too tight for his face. He was completely bald and had no facial hair,a little above average height, and was wearing a full tracksuit of cyan blue. Before he even said a word I assumed he must have been some eccentric tech millionaire based off of this dress alone, the kind of money that for some reason always eliminates good taste. When he introduced himself, he was very soft spoken.

"You seem a little forlorn, don't you?"

I was unaccustomed to being approached or evaluated by strangers, especially so dressed, and it took me a second to get my bearings. "No, not at all. I'm just thinking."

"Oh? About illegal dog fighting, maybe?"

My face must have shown some mixture of shame or surprise, because he laughed. "Don't worry, I'm listening too. It's fascinating stuff, really, isn't it? Do you own any dogs?"

"I...no, I do not."

"Such a shame. A man should be so lucky to have a companion for this world."

"...I'm guessing that you own – "

"Yes, a border collie," he beamed, "I've had him since he was a pup. Name's Maxwell. He's getting on in years though, the old boy." He looked a little sad for a split second.

"And have you ever thought of dog fighting?" I asked.

"Me?" He looked genuinely offended, but this too lasted for only a moment. He laughed. "Not once, never. I can't imagine the cruelty of such owners. Do you think that, uh...?" He gestured downwards.

"I don't think so, no. It sounds like they're discussing the ways by which dogs are trained, but I've also heard them discount it as barbaric."

"Well, that's a relief, then. I'd hate to share space with people like that." A moment of silence, then he held out his hand. "Stephen."

I hesitated, but shook it and gave him a false name.

"What do you do, are you a student?"

"Not anymore. I'm currently looking for work." This was partially true. I didn't want the online publishing thing to last longer than necessary, and I had been playing around with the idea of reapplying for more jobs to start once my apartment was acquired.

With a sagely nod he approved. "I gotcha. It's not easy, especially in a big city."

"No, it is not. What is it you do?"

"Oh, I'm semi-retired myself." He leaned back in his chair.

We both looked out onto the bay for a moment as a small boat lingered by near the middle. A figure near the stern was repeatedly tossing and reeling in a fishing line. I was going over in my head what exactly this guy's deal was but wondered if he was just being friendly and I was acting the odd one out. The sun was close to setting now, and I could hear the people below us shifting in their chairs as they prepared to leave.

"Well, there goes our entertainment," said Stephen. Now he hesitated for a moment. "Say, why not join me at my place? I live not too far from here. I can't stand closed little bars like this, honestly. I like more familiar spaces, open spaces."

If my guard had started to lower before it was back up in an instant. This invitation made me fairly uncomfortable, and I don't think I need to explain why. I didn't hesitate to point out the fact that we had spoken for perhaps only a minute. "I don't think so. Not to say anything against you, but we don't know each other at all. I think I'll stay."

His face fell, and what had been a consistently pleased look turned to a supremely tired one.

"It's a sad day and age when a man cannot invite another to his home for fear of better knowing him."

The manner in which he pronounced this, so incredibly melodramatic, somehow seemed genuine, and I felt for a moment embarrassed of myself for having doubted his sincerity. Naturally such a proclamation would have sounded ridiculous in regular conversation, but for some reason – maybe it was his mannerisms or the way he presented himself, or the meeting as a whole – saying something like that seemed completely appropriate for someone like him. After all, wasn't this the kind of interaction I had expected or even hoped for by frequenting a place like this? Did I really think this guy was dangerous or something? I reconsidered, then reluctantly retracted my answer.

"Great!" He smiled again, as if expecting me to change my mind. He got up at once, and after a second I followed, completely unsure of whether I was making a wise choice. Actually, I most certainly wasn't, but that had never seemed to hinder me before.

We got to the parking lot and I followed him in my modest truck as he drove his Cadillac, which was unashamedly the same color of the clothing he wore, through roads and bright night lights. The moon and bay remained on our left until we turned inland and drove several miles further, deeper into the hills that California is pebbled with, that slope into valleys and crevices born of soft, tan mounds that hide away the secret cradles of new and old millionaires. We passed by several ornate gates and glimpses of private monuments as we made our way curving and weaving into and over hills, until finally we made a turn at the summit of one of them, and we were there.

Stephen's own home was as glamorous as the ones we had passed on our sojourn to it, but it was smaller in stature. The mansion was white and gold, Grecian pillars adorning both the front and back porch, and with half-cylinder tiles of beige lining the roof. To the south a ways was the beginnings of the all-too-necessary vineyard, which he sheepishly pointed out as we entered.

"Kind of a hobby I once picked up and never bothered to maintain. I should just tear the thing down and lay off all of the folks who I pay for the upkeep, but it's got a bit of a charm, I think."

Opening the front door he was assailed by a black and white blur which shot like a bullet from the threshold and jumped excitedly on old paws. Stephen laughed and introduced me to Maxwell, who then turned his interest to me. Maxwell followed as I was led through to the back porch of the house, which gave a fine view of the San Francisco skyline, now much further away. The sun was setting, and brilliant orange and pink reflections were clear on the uppermost windows of the city's tallest skyscrapers as the sun made its descent into the ocean.

Stephen invited me to seat myself in one of two wicker chairs paired side-by-side, and retreated into the kitchen. His backyard ended suddenly at the bottom of a soft slope of well-tended grass, at the foot of a brick wall which enclosed the entirety of his courtyard. This far away from the city or suburban life, it was serenely quiet. The only sounds now were the breeze, and some far off birds calling to one another as the day drew to a close. If you listened closely enough, you could hear old straw rope pulling and tugging in the wind as it struggled in the neglected vineyard not so far away with thick vines and heavy grapes.

Stephen returned momentarily with two whiskeys, and a box of cigars, to which I declined. "Good man," He said, closing the lid but with one of the cigars, unlit, between his teeth. "Awful habit."

Maxwell had taken a seat at the arm of his master, who simply sat and drank in contentment for a moment. He had not hung up his tracksuit jacket or relinquished any of the costume which he had adorned himself with. He could easily be seated back in the bar where we had met, save for the fact that he was clearly more at ease. He pulled a little gold lighter out from somewhere, lit his cigar, and inhaled deeply.

"This is much, much better." He let out a huge cloud of smoke, and I agreed.

"Do you always invite strangers you meet to come home with you?"

"Yes," he replied, seriously. "But very rarely is my offer taken. Is it so hard to believe a man simply wants to drink and converse in the comfort of his own home?"

"Well...don't you have any friends of your own?" I regretted saying it like this, but he laughed.

"Yes, but I like to meet new people. What's a shame is that women who tend to come home with me expect that I'm trying to pull something with them."

"Wouldn't most people?"

"I dislike that that's the case," he shifted in his chair.

I hadn't seen a ring on his finger. "No desire to get married? You must get lonely out here."

"Well, that's true." He patted Maxwell's head, whose tail slapped once or twice lazily against the ground in response. "And that's part of the reason I go out to meet people. But, as for something like that, well, no."

"There are no women at all in your life?"

"None," he sniffed. Then, he hesitated for a moment. "I don't, ah..."

He cleared his throat and continued, looking straight ahead. "...don't really like to have sex. It's as if we're eager...I don't know, to forsake our own innocence, at the cost of some physical intimacy."

This instantly annoyed me to such an extent that I considered getting up and leaving without another word. Another absurd, far-too-intimate self-possessed proclamation which left a tangible silence in the moments that followed, and I just sat by awkwardly and pretended that perhaps he hadn't said anything at all. I could see now that I was expected to be held captive while some stranger played out his adolescent personal doctrine built from who knows what experiences, possibly for my validation. I was reminded of college.

The conversation eventually returned to earthly topics which could be indulged in without any sort of heartfelt admission. I admit that I resented him slightly for opening up as such, as I had had no desire at all to gain that uncomfortable knowledge, but I noticed that after this, his demeanor had changed. With no response from me, he put on a façade. We continued to discuss our mutual lives and habits (to a point – as always I didn't disclose anything potentially dangerous), but I sensed that he was bored, and was ultimately disappointed in something. While I felt only slightly bad for possibly letting him down, I was not eager to have him unveil his universal values to me, no matter how alien he may have seemed. But this didn't matter, as he finally broke all customary social boundaries and straight-out asked me, as we were discussing something along the lines of California beaches, what I believed in.

"And I'm not referring to religion, necessarily," he clarified, pouring himself another glass. "I'm wondering if you have any personal truths, something that drives you. I've shared one of mine."

"Stephen..."

"Indulge me. It's so rare someone comes this far."

I hated these types of conversations because they are nothing more than mental masturbation, meant to sate one's own belief that, beneath their exterior skin of being as everyone else, they were philosophers. Under the guise of learning from one another and approaching some sort of shared nirvana was the truth that they were comparing themselves and stroking their ego. These were the types of things people discussed in puberty, not as fully grown adult men.

"I believe in nothing in particular."

"Come on."

"Not everyone has something so profound saved up to say at a moment's notice." This was a kind of dig at him, but if he got it he ignored it.

"You've nothing to wake up to in the morning? Nothing drives you?"

"I'm sure something does. But I just can't name it. Maybe someday I'll be able to." Then, remembering our age difference, and desperately hoping to change the topic, "I'm still young, you know."

This seemed to sate him. The moon was overhead now, and he looked up at it for a few moments, contemplating. Maxwell had fallen asleep. Towards the end of his courtyard began the blinking of fireflies in the darkness.

He nodded, once. "That's not perfect, but it works. Thank you."

"Why so interested?"

"Honestly? Just curiosity. Sometimes I'm worried that I'm really strange."

My frustration had mostly subsided by now. At least he was self-aware. "You're pretty strange. But I've met stranger, if it helps." He laughed.

"You'll be leaving soon?"

"Yes, I think so. Thank you for a pleasant evening."

"Thank you for the same."

I got up and walked back towards the house, making my way to the driveway. I turned back once to look at him, and saw him silhouetted in the darkness of the evening, the fireflies now dancing around his domain, a glass to his lips, cigar between his fingers, and eyes to the sky.

Chapter 5

After my meeting with Stephen, I was reassured of my initial feelings towards the bar, and had no qualms about frequenting the place more and more often. Stephen did not return there. However, a few weeks after having met him, several things happened at once.

First and foremost, without any sort of reason given, the price of the apartment I had had my eye on decreased. I had no idea why at the time, but I quickly took advantage of the situation, and immediately moved out of my grandmother's flat to my new home. The following days were spent buying cheap furniture at flea markets or at garage sales or secondhand stores and tossing them into my truck to furnish my sanctuary. It was pleasant, and almost just as I had imagined: on the third floor, to the right of the stairwell was my door – big, brass numbers screwed into the wood, under the small eyehole – and opening it, you'd find yourself in the living room, which was adjacent immediately to the dining area, all in an open space. A single, long couch, a small television with a stand, and a round oak table with folding chairs placed around it. To the left of the dining area, in a small room which made up the wall immediately to the left of the entrance door, was the kitchen. Nothing too spectacular. An old fridge, a stove, a sink which sometimes ran no water, and cupboards on rusty hinges and stained linoleum.

Past the living room, down a hallway immediately straight ahead of the entrance, was a bathroom on the right-hand side, and a closet across from it. At the end of the hall was my bedroom, and with it its own bathroom and closet. I had windows all around – one behind the T.V., one above the sink in the kitchen, and one large one in my bedroom to the right of my bed, facing the street.

The most important feature, however, was the balcony, the single, sole attraction which had swayed me to wait and save up my earnings to inhabit this otherwise lonely little place. Behind the dining room table was a sliding glass door, which led out onto a small wooden pad, and gave me my view of the bay and the city which it hugged. Below me was a long line of rocks and sand, stretching all the way down the coastline in either direction, which the surf crashed on in rhythmic, endless patterns, and could be heard even with the door shut.

The entire process of moving took around a week of my time, including placing the furniture in all the right places and sometimes hiring help to bring the bigger pieces in, but in the end, I was finally alone in a place I was the master of, free of all company and other people. I now had the autonomy to choose my life. I could remain indoors, or I could, if I wanted the company, go out and seek it – via endless gallery cruising along the highway, or silent listening in my latest fascination, the bar.

The question now arose, however, of my business regarding the source of my income, now that I had made the money to move where I wanted. Did I want to continue working the way that I had, publishing nonsense that shadows seemed to eat up and spew out money in return? Of course not. It was dangerous work. Sensationalist writings for whomever was gobbling them up so eagerly was not the type of career I had seen for myself, if indeed I had seen one at all. No, it hinged too much on the current of the times, it was too unreliable and I was convinced that it could one day prove to be fatal, given the correct circumstances.

But the biggest problem challenging my note of resignation was the simple matter of employment. I had no other ventures I could pursue. This problem plagued my mind occasionally, until one day, perhaps not only a few days after the moving business had concluded, I came across the reason why the pricing of my apartment had fallen, and I was temporarily distracted.

An unfortunate malady within the piping of my apartment and my apartment alone in the whole building caused my water to turn brown at least twice a week for several hours. I discovered this while showering, and thought that perhaps I had gone colorblind, or that I was suddenly bathing in dirt. The landlord refused to assist in the matter, citing that lowering the price of the apartment cleared him of all responsibility by some inane logic, and thus I was forced to look for a plumber myself. I called the cheapest one available, and this was how I met Don.

Don appeared at my door the same day I called him, dressed in a bright red jumpsuit, carrying a toolbox, and resembling something akin to a propaganda poster for American industrialism in the WWII era. He was bald, fat, and his hands were almost nothing but callouses, white, blistering bulbs of work that moved like individual muscles on each knuckle. I explained the situation to him as he went about inspecting the piping of my sink.

"And the landlord won't help you?"

"Not one bit."

"God, that's shitty. These same people had me come by another one of their buildings and clear out a rat infestation, and did the same thing to the guys over there."

"No kidding?"

"Claimed it was due to the poor hygiene of the tenants living there. Poor hygiene! Can you imagine? What a fucking slap in the face."

Eventually, it was discovered that the issue was in the basement of the building itself, or at least it had to be, as there was no single cause for my water dirtying within my apartment. This forced the landlord, a wild-haired man with a thin, dirty tie and loose suit, to angrily drive up, give a few words to both Don and I, and give Don the key to the basement with the agreement to return it to his office downtown. As he drove off, Don burst out laughing.

"He gave me the same key for the last place I worked at too, the one with the rats? These idiots don't change the locks on their buildings, and I still have the key from there."

"So there was no need for him to come? You have a key for the basement?"

"Yeah, but I wanted to get him back. Can't stand the guy." I decided that I liked my plumber.

The problem, after a thorough inspection of the basement, turned out to be quite complicated, and involved outdated systems within the complex that the landlord or whoever actually ran these apartments had "forgotten" to have updated to save costs. The issue was so serious that Don had to call an entire team down to the building, and soon enough at least five large middle-aged men in a rainbow of jumpsuits were hammering away loudly down below for a week. Feeling sorry for them, I one day brought down soda, penetrating an orchestra of steaming valves and clanging metal amongst swearing.

"This is company neglect if I've ever seen it (thank you)," Don said, wiping his brow his sleeve and drinking deep from the can of Sprite. "It gets worse every time we get deeper into it. If you hadn't called us when you had, this would have happened to other apartments here, and soon enough it would have turned poisonous."

"It wasn't already?"

"Poisonous? No, not yet. You see that valve over there?" He pointed to a small pipe across the basement, where a man in blue and a man in orange were looking over a blueprint nearby. "Long story short, that needed to be replaced about five years ago."

"How much is this operation going to cost me?" I asked. My heart was sinking at the circus of sweltering, disgruntled men and exposed construction.

"Oh no, *you* ain't payin'," Don gave a hearty laugh, which rippled throughout his fat stomach. "When I told our boss back at the office about this, she got *so* mad – the city's suin' your landlord and whoever he works for over this. This is a public hazard, citizens could've been hospitalized over this because they didn't wanna update their systems." I was incredibly relieved, and pleasantly surprised. Sure enough, my neighbors and I received a letter from our landlord a few days later formally apologizing for the affair and explaining in detail the issues which my employed plumbers were handling, all the while conveniently avoiding the fact that it was entirely his fault. As the main portion of the work was done, Don, who had been first on call for the repairs, was relegated to overseer, and thus had little more to do than watch his coworkers handle the remnants of the plumbing for the last few days. During this time, I invited him to use my apartment to do his paperwork.

"Nothin's left to be said," he stated, looking over his documents at my dining table, wearing a pair of large reading glasses. A thin little chain connected both ends of them and were drawn behind his neck, getting lost in the folds of his skin. "There was no contest. If they didn't acquiesce, they might've been shut down by the city, so they quickly admitted and paid us what we were due, and then some. Slimy bastards," he added, "I almost wanted to see them get gutted. But I don't think they'll try pulling something like this again."

I found myself not wanting our time together to end, for some reason. Maybe it was his blunt personality, or the fact that it was real human interaction, but Don was at the very least entertaining and not stupid. So when the time came for him and his cohorts to pack up and leave, I walked up to him as he was departing my apartment and asked if I could buy him a beer, in thanks. I didn't know how else to approach him, and whether or not this was awkward, or if he got the wrong idea. But, after recovering – his eyebrows had darted upwards – he laughed again.

"Yeah, why not? Where were you thinking?"

"I know this little bar down the way."

"Lemme give you my number. I'm free on...uh, Saturday. I'll call ya then." And he left.

This was good news, as I hadn't made any real acquaintances since coming to Berkeley, and while our meeting was by no means indicative of whether or not a friendship of some kind would follow, that Don agreed to indulge me showed that he wouldn't mind at least seeing if we were compatible outside of him loudly working in my apartment. However, the following day after the chaos of the plumbing ended, I received a call from a friend of my grandmother's, whose message I could barely make out through her tears. She had died.

They found her while bringing some groceries over to the apartment, face down in the kitchen, a cup of coffee shattered on the porcelain, dead of what seemed to be a heart attack. This had happened only a day ago, and only about a week and a half after I had moved out. I was informed that I had been included in the will, and was to be given the vast majority of her savings, no small amount. Though it potentially could have fallen to me to be the executor of her estate, and thus have had the responsibility of handling the colossal paperwork, I was very relieved when her friends offered to handle it, thinking that I was a poor and very busy young man. So while the funeral arrangements were being taken care of, my plans with Don remained uninterrupted, and I received a nice bundle of money as well. There would be time for grief at the appropriate time and place.

"Fold."

"I see your ten."

"Right, that's the last round, right?"

"Right. Okay, so show us your cards…"

This was the conversation that greeted me as I waited for Don the following Saturday. It was held between the three young men who frequented the bar almost daily and held a small corner near the window of the ground floor as their meeting area. Two of them were attempting to teach the third how to play poker.

"Why did you keep betting?" The largest of the three, named George, clearly an athlete of some sort, asked. He showed signs of balding and wearing a white tank top. "You've got literally nothing. There isn't any way this hand could have won."

"But I've got the uh, the king. Right? Isn't that good?" The one they were trying to teach looked even more confused. His name was Walker, and he had long, straight blonde hair and was clearly very thin despite wearing for some reason a very loose sweater. He had either forgotten to shave or was trying to grow a beard and was failing, as it dotted his chin and cheeks in uneven yellow patches. Hung over the back of his chair was a backpack covered in buttons and pins.

"No, you need more than just one face card. It needs to match with something else somehow." The last of the trio, Louis, chimed in. He was somewhere between the two in size, and his hair was short and black. He wore glasses and a red sweatshirt. And he was being much more patient with his friend than George was.

"Okay! Okay. No worries. I'll try again. Try to match them, right?"

"Yes. Okay, I'll deal."

A moment of shuffling and the sound of cards being handed out.

"Okay, now ante up."

"What's that mean again?"

"Walker, it's the *third hand*." George finally got a little exasperated.

The door opened and Don appeared in the entryway like a boulder blocking out the sun, and I waved him over. He was eyeing the place and sauntered to the back corner with a look that seemed like approval.

"Cozy little place, isn't it?" He sat down very heavily, his girth making the chair squeak as he nestled himself in. "Never heard if this place before. What's it called?"

"It doesn't have a name, I think. Just a bar." He was still dressed in his plumbing jumpsuit. He must have just come from a job. "I owe you a beer."

"Yes! Yes you do," he laughed, and turned as if to call the bartender over to us. I stopped him.

"They don't come to the tables here. What'll you have?"

I returned with a few beers and found that he had been listening very intently to the conversation between the three young men, as I had. Things had not gotten better and the largest of the three had started to become very red in the face with frustration.

"How do you get to that age and not know how to play poker? That blonde one's as thick as a brick," he added under his breath.

With a guest now present, I began to notice the flaws of what had been my personal garden of Eden with much more clarity. The peeling of splinters on the old wooden walls, the musky smell that arose from the floorboards every morning, the lighting, and so on. In the same moment I was both worried and relieved when my mind went to the more embarrassing regulars, and remembered that Eddie had already come in and tried to sell his "catch" earlier, and the student of pornography was busy studying for finals. I had overheard him discuss this earlier this week with another student, a friend who was apparently undeterred by his hobby. Even the young Asian girl had her headphones on upstairs.

"So, what's your deal anyways? You're a student I'm guessing, right?" Don brought me back to life after a moment of silence.

"No, I – I was, but college didn't really work out for me. I'm a freelance author right now."

"No worries, kid. College ain't for everyone."

"It certainly isn't."

Our conversation went very smoothly, as it turned out. Don was very personable, and either feigned interest very well, or genuinely found me interesting to an extent. He had been a plumber for thirty years, and had lived in the bay area for twenty. He had a penchant for whisky, and loved blues, especially anything that focused on the harmonica as the focal point. He also had a family, a crumpled picture of which he had plastered in his wallet.

"This is my lovely gal, Adelaide. Met her in High school." *Adelaide.* There was a name you never heard. He pointed to a portly woman with a modest hairstyle tied up in a bow, and whose face, with a small smile, radiated matronly beauty – a woman who had once been gorgeous, and had transitioned into motherhood with a sort of wise serenity. Seated next to her was Don, dressed messily in a suit and tie and grinning wildly like he couldn't believe his luck. Next to him was a young boy and two girls. Jason, his son who couldn't have been more than ten in the photo, was crowned with an enormous brown cowlick that had been evidently attacked with hair gel and cream, but was given up upon, and as a result it sat on his head like some sad brown flying saucer. He was dressed in a neatly pressed tuxedo. The two girls, Jordan and Isabelle, were obviously twins, dressed in matching polka-dot dresses. Their long, curly hair was tied back with a large bow, and they seemed the most sheepish, looking downwards in embarrassment in front of the camera. All of the children were mimicking their father's wild grin.

"That's a beautiful family." He nodded and put his wallet away. At this point in our conversation, a young man I had not seen before, dressed in a lime-green knit sweater vest that hugged him a little too tightly, walked over to the damnable jukebox that had rested silently thus far, and turned it on. I wished internally that it would be music, which was oh-so-rare here, but my wishes were not met. Some voice began to droll something out from the speakers, and the young man, nodding to himself, walked back to his seat:

...Rejoice,
rejoice,
now

Whatever Don had been saying soon trailed off as his ears registered what it was that he was hearing. He turned to look at the jukebox, now glowing in green and blue neon, and turned back to me, and then to the jukebox again. I was very worried that he'd be put off by something like that – which would be totally understandable – but he turned back to me, with a look of bewilderment, and said

"Holy shit. That's hilarious."

"Yes," I gave a sigh of relief and finished the last of my beer. "it really is." In a moment, Don and I were friends.

<u>Chapter 6</u>

Our relationship started out a little awkwardly, as one could expect, but in truth, Don and I were extremely compatible. It was after our initial meeting that he began to feel more comfortable, and he saw something in me that drew him towards my companionship. I know now that he had made the fatal error of assuming that I was a "soft-spoken" type, which adhered to a masculinity he deemed appropriate for all young men in that I did not speak unless I had something to say, as he termed it once. He really liked that. We met up more and more often, and he introduced me to pastimes I had absolutely no interest in, such as golfing, or working on cars. When he found out that I especially did not care much about the latter, he slapped his forehead and lamented: "And do you know what you're driving?"

But I digress. I mentioned that my problem of finding more desirable employment was interrupted by Don's arrival into my life. Around a month after we had met and formally begun our friendship, I brought the subject up once while he and I were smacking golf balls aimlessly one afternoon. He looked quite a sight, the large, sweaty man, focus crinkling his brow and dressed, obliviously, in a filthy jumpsuit, as he swung mightily in the proximity of what must have been heirs and prodigies. He immediately offered me a position with his company.

"I'll talk to a few of my guys, but we'll find a place for gruntwork. Always need more of that." I was freed in a sentence. That same day, I floated home and curtly cut ties with my publisher, giving no explanation aside from the simple fact that I no longer wanted to do it. They sent me several responses, alarmed, pleading me to return. They offered me a raise, two raises, a change in alias, a change in deadlines. But I ignored them all.

On the eve of the following day, I was driving by my grandmother's old place, and saw that there was a crowd of onlookers gathering around the bottom floor. I stopped, and got out.

They were all looking up at something, the window to our old apartment. There was an enormous hole in the glass. Spotting the owner of the grocery store below – a man with wispy gray hair and beady, black eyes – I approached him.

"What happened here?" He didn't recognize me. I had rarely shopped for myself when living above him.

"No idea. Heard a crash about ten minutes ago, then a car sped off."

I pondered the sight for a moment, then left to resume my route. It would come out later that a brick had been thrown into the building, with a note attached. What this note detailed was not included in the news story.

Maybe it was the exciting change in occupation, but I found myself appreciating, though not exactly enjoying my new job. There's something to be said about working with your hands, putting in real, genuine hours as opposed to writing some nonsense once in a while and sending it off. Here I saw the fruits of my labor, from the smallest clogged faucet to something more complex, like an industrial malfunction. I was put alongside Don as a sort of instructor/partner, as he was the one who spoke for me and got me the position. This led to he and I working on numerous calls together, and we ended up spending more time than ever in each other's company.

Don, as it turned out, was a man prone to pointless musings. These were especially prevalent during hours that did not so much require focus and planning, but rather simple, repetitive manual labor. As I have previously mentioned, I am not a fan of what I considered superfluous arguments and reflections. I made this clear to my colleague/trainer, and yet all the same he would bring some thought or idea up while tightening a screw or replacing a pipe. At the very least, he was someone whose appearance and age could forgive this meandering daydreaming, and in order to appease his appetite for competitive contemplation, I would at one point or another give in to his meditations. He knew full well that I was answering only to humor him, but that did not necessarily mean that I was being fictitious. We were becoming friends, and it was my duty to indulge him.

One discussion came during a memorable call to a public pool, not too far from Berkeley. Upon arriving, we were told that a skunk had managed to get past the chain-link fence and had drowned overnight in the water. Moreover, he had sunk to the bottom of the deep end. And the pole that tends to be at public pools to clean up leaves and the like would not be strong enough to lift the animal out.

"This presents several logistical problems," said Don, pacing back and forth around the water's edge, hands clasped behind his back like some professor mulling over a difficult equation. "How do we get the thing out of here, firstly: and second, how to clean the pool floor where he's been laying?" A slight green and red haze had formed around the sad and deflated shape of the creature as it drifted far below the surface. Part of our contract was to disinfect the pool as well, or at least, sterilize the area the skunk had died in.

"Someone's going to have to go in and get it." I had no illusions that the unfortunate person to perform this would be me – new on the job and all of that. Don nodded sagely, then, furrowing his brow, shook his head.

"We've got no diving equipment." This was true, and presented a problem. I was not going to dive into those contaminated waters without protection.

Eventually, we came to a compromise of ideas: rather than sacrifice some poor soul (me) to dive in and retrieve the corpse, we instead pushed the skunk using the net up to the shallow end, and sort of scrapped it up to the point where a heavily gloved hand (mine) could grab it. This solved that quandary, but our task resulted in a trail of blood and death clearly traced from the center of the deep end, upwards the slope to the shallow, and then end in a sharp ninety degree angle onto the wall of the pool. Thankfully, our company did have the proper heavy equipment to deal with this, so for the rest of the day, Don and I switched roles from guiding a large machine which scrambled on the pool floor to clean it. I anticipated that with such mindless work a bored Don would soon find his brain wandering, and soon enough, he began to voice aloud his ruminations.

"Y'know what's interesting?" He was sat lounging in a pool chair while I took my turn steering the machine.

"What's that."

"I was one of the last people I know to get married. All of my buddies got hitched way before I did."

"Mmm."

"It kinda bothers me, though," He sat up with a grunt, "Why do people feel like they need to marry so young? I mean, you really think you've found the, the love of your life by what, twenty five?"

"A lot of your friends divorced, then?"

A pause. "No," he lay back down, pondering. "No, they're not. A few, but not most of 'em."

I thought foolishly that perhaps I had avoided it, but then:

"The question remains!" He sat back up. "Most people marry young. Out of college, or in college, even. Why do you think that is?"

"They're in love?"

"How do they really know that? So young, you don't think that it might be better to wait a few years, see the world, explore?"

"You're basing this…on the pretense that all relationships…follow a similar path," I turned the machine to guide it up the wall. "People who marry young may well have had plenty of relationships before, or maybe they don't see the need to look for more when they're perfectly happy as is."

"There's something more, and you know it. Why do people want to marry at all?"

"What? I – children, love?"

"*Loneliness.*"

"Oh, come on. It's your turn." I tried to distract him by doing this, but he just sauntered up and laughed while I took his spot on the chair.

"I didn't need to find someone so young! I took my time, y'know. Enjoyed myself, then found the right girl – even though we'd met in high school. Funny, that. How many girlfriends have you had, kiddo?"

"None."

"None?"

"No."

"And why is that?"

"I don't know."

"None of the tail at Berkeley suited you, huh?"

The truth was that I thought it was all too much work. But I just said "I don't know. I've never been really attracted to anyone."

"Oh. I, uh...are you gay?"

"No."

"Well..." A few moments of respite. "No one, huh?"

"Again, Don, no."

"Come on," he forced a laugh, "You don't want to find some girl, get out there, and have some fun?"

"I don't, Don."

"Oh stop it, you're a young man. Of course you're interested in women."

I didn't know how else to respond to him, so I just stared at the clouds. It would probably rain later, so hopefully we could finish this all up soon. Out of the corner of my eye I saw his smile fade, and he looked back down to the machine as it worked. I almost think he was embarrassed. He did not bring up the topic again for the rest of the day.

I did not stop frequenting the bar, if I need to say it. My second home remained as such regardless of my change in career, and things there stayed the same. Still the young blonde man openly read porn at the windowsill, still the art teacher scowled, and sometimes, greatly daring, confronted him to no end result. Still young Benjamin and Katie visited and took up the couch upstairs – still the deadly Asian girl stopped their romances with jarring electro-house. Still Eddie tried to sell old fish to the bartender every Monday morning. And still sat the three young men at their table downstairs, and had their discussions and muses. This was where I now felt the most comfortable. I knew each of these people almost intimately, and yet, not a single one of them even took notice of who I was. It was perfect. The question of why I derived so much pleasure out of watching these people bit at the back of my skull, and I did inwardly groan whenever someone would activate that detestable jukebox, but I ignored the former and bore the latter. What did that matter, as long as I was gaining something - even if I didn't know what that was - out of it all?

I had been employed with Don for around a month when we were asked to take on some work at an office building in downtown San Francisco along with a few other teams from our little outfit. This particular job required a more experienced hand, and I was really just there to fetch things. Don has been once again relegated to task leader, and has in front of him a large blueprint of the facility at all hours of the day.

I do not go downtown often, for reasons of privacy. Like any big city, San Francisco is too dirty, too loud and too crowded for me to find any enjoyment out of being in it, much less injected directly into its metropolitan heart. I let my guard down as I thought it very unlikely that someone within this building or outside of it would catch a glimpse of me and connect me with some news story months ago. Thankfully, no one shouted my name or rushed at me, faceless and ignored in the background of bustling metropolis life.

San Francisco is also too cold a city in the summertime. Great gusts of wind come sweeping down over postcard hills and make a mess the hair of young women, shuddering their Sunday skirts and billowing like great invisible snakes past cars and precarious apartment complexes. The wind on the worst days is deafening with the force of the Pacific current behind it, and as we're working it almost seizes Don's blueprints from him several times, eliciting a feverish swear that increases in viciousness with each attempt. We spend the entire day downtown, being pushed side to side by the blows, until finally we manage to complete our task, and each worker quickly sets off to evacuate the frigid sidewalks.

"Hey, you doin' anything tonight?" Don called to me as I entered my truck.

"No, why?"

"Well, why not come by my place for dinner? The wife's making a pot roast, and we can never finish the whole thing. Plus you can meet the kids."

I was not aware that I was eligible for such an honor, but for the free meal, I acquiesced. I followed him home for the first time, a long drive away (leaving the city is always a long drive), and found that he lived not too far from the Claremont, in a small – but respectable – place hidden behind a general store, titled in heavily outdated neon *Adam and Jane's Wares*. Don's house was situated side-by-side the parking lot of this store, and it seemed terribly out of place.

A large wooden porch and a low overhanging roof made the large structure seem more at-home in a bayou setting than some alleyway in California. The windows were the kind of melted glass you see only in really old buildings, and here and there the green creep of rot bled from the corners of dark paneling. Despite all of this, it was unquestionably a home with as much personality as its owner.

This would be magnified to a much greater extent upon entering, where I was greeted with a labyrinth of knickknacks and novelties that I could not properly describe because of their sheer numeracy and uniqueness. This was a collection, I would later learn, of curiosities that Don and his wife had procured over a long span of time from antique stores, garage sales, flea markets and the like. It reached the ceiling and was very stifling, but clearly it had all been laid out with respect and care. You had to squeeze by different routes, depending on where you wanted to go – take a left at the large statue of the Indian woman breastfeeding her twins to reach the kitchen, or a right at the collection of leather-bound Venetian amateur screenplays sat upon a small end table made of walrus bone for the bathroom. The dining room was situated between two separate, open cabinets of handmade origin that displayed within them various jewelry and paintings, paintings made by children or experienced professionals sat side-by-side. Thankfully, only the front room was filled as such, and the rest of Don's modest home was strikingly normal in contrast. I was a little dizzy as I sat down at the table, and for a moment did not recognize that someone was sitting across from me. Don's wife was beaming at me with a friendliness that almost made me uncomfortable, with such intensity that I mistook it for barely-withheld pity. But I came to the conclusion later that evening that she was simply a very kind woman.

The dinner was, as advertised, delicious and plentiful, and conversation was light. I was introduced to Adelaide and Don's children as a co-worker, and it was here that I realized that Don's picture in his wallet must have been quite old. His wife had more wrinkles, and his children were much taller and less smiley. Not to say that they were not polite or pleasant, but, like teenagers, they took little notice of me as food was placed on the table.

Adelaide was a very pleasant lady, who was wearing a scarf on her head like you'd see in pictures of Russian *babushkas*. A navy apron covered her wide midriff, and she was smiling for the entirety of the meal.

"Where do you go to school, dear? You look awfully young to be hanging around Don's Old Men's Club."

"I'm a dirty dropout. College didn't work for me, but things are going very well."

"All he does is drink all day down at some bar," Don chimed in, a mouth half-full of steaming vegetables. "Gets his kicks outta eavesdropping."

"We all have our hobbies. That place would crumble without me. Think of how much money I've given them."

It went on like this. Shallow, but not unpleasant conversation. Things were going smoothly, yet disaster peaked on the horizon for one unfathomable instant as I realized that Don's son had been staring intently at me from the far end of the table. I ventured a small smile at him, but it was not reciprocated. Instead, deadpan, and in the pause of chatter, he said

"I think I've seen you on T.V. before."

Conversation stopped for what felt like eons, but in reality must have been three or four seconds. Yet, to my own surprise, I handled the danger with much more ease and poise than I thought I would.

"When I was a kid and wore glasses, people used to say I looked like Harry Potter."

Don choked while laughing, adding to the distraction. Harry Potter. Where did that come from? I'd never even needed glasses, but I confused him and deterred him from encroaching on forbidden land. And yet, his eyebrows came together in what must have been some internal perplexity. My mind flashed back to the mural that I had stumbled across months ago, but that was far away from here.

The dinner finished soon thereafter, and Don's children slinked away. His daughters hadn't said a word to me throughout, talking amongst themselves, which was preferable. When I picked up my plate to take it into the kitchen, Don's wife slapped my hand.

"You stop that. I'll take care of the dishes." And she sauntered off with a tower cupped under her hands.

Don had been drinking a little, and was now messing with an old record player in the far corner of the room. He hadn't removed his jumpsuit, even at the table, and he glowed like some great red sun in the setting light of the day from the window behind him, foot tapping to some internal tune.

Eventually he found what he was looking for, popped it in, carefully dropped the needle, and soon the loud trumpets of some upbeat song called *Papa Loves Mambo* by Perry Como came on. His hips shook with jerky movements as he helped bring the dishes into the kitchen.

"Grab a dish or two, you lazy freeloader," he said in good spirits, humming to himself the tune. I didn't argue, and we began to ferry to and fro.

At some point in the song he began to sing the chorus.

"Mama's looking for papa, but papa's nowhere in *sight*!"

"You've got it wrong," Adelaide called from the kitchen. "It's '*Papa's* looking for *mama,* but *mama* is nowhere in sight." But Don didn't answer, humming happily to himself.

<u>Chapter 7</u>

Eventually the table was cleared, and Don called me out onto the porch for a few drinks. I had seen the rocking chairs on the way in, and thought that they had looked rather inviting, so I happily obliged, despite having to venture through that obscure bazaar in order to get there. We sat in silence for a little while, looking over the black tar of the small parking lot that was his front yard, and it came to me that perhaps I had been a little too hasty to judge this location on first impression. The area was completely boxed in by surrounding buildings, not too tall, and it was peacefully quiet. Only a few cars and trucks were here and there, the last customers of *Adam and Jane's*, and the setting sun painted very brightly a nice canvas of pink above the roofs of the building directly across from us. Even with Don's son glaring somewhere in the back of my mind, I was overall pleased with the way the evening had turned out.

"I've been doing this all of my life," Don said after a few minutes more of musing. I heard the beer swish as he lifted the bottle up to his mouth again. "Plumbing and all of that. Did it to make money for myself, wasted it on things. I didn't care. And then I got married. And then I had kids. And now I'm here. It's all gone according to plan – I've always been in control, from the beginning to now. That's the way, the way I think life aughta be lived. You should know fully well what your day tomorrow will be like, and the next, and the next, and forever."

He was speaking to the parking lot, but if he'd turn to look at me I can't imagine how surprised I must have looked. This little revelation may have been spurred by alcohol, and to some ears it may have been alarming, but if ever there was one conversation that solidified my faith in Don, it was this one. It is the one I remember clearest, and reflect on the most, despite what would eventually happen between us. I did not only agree with him, he had expressed in a few words what I had always held to be true. I left soon thereafter, but I did so with a greater respect for the man who I had only so long ago called to complain about building maintenance.

This evening did have some negative side effects in that I was now formally introduced to Don's family. This meant that meetings could become more infrequent, and the fact that Don's sharp kid had recognized me on T.V. from first sight meant that he could not be dissuaded forever. These fears were realized one morning when, only a week later, I received a call from Don, asking me a huge favor. His son had baseball practice in some park somewhere, but both Don and his wife were indisposed.

"I'll pay ya gas money, I just really need your help."

"There's no-one else you could call to do this?" Unspoken social norms would argue that I should have taken the favor regardless, but I was wary. The prolonged amount of time alone with Don's son was something I did not want to put myself through.

"There really isn't. Please, I'm begging you."

Annoyed, I conceded, and drove over to pick up his son, dressed in his baseball uniform and waiting for me on the deck of his *Deliverance*-esque home. Wordlessly he got in, and I vainly hoped that he would remain silent out of awkwardness throughout the ride. This was inevitably not the case, as maybe five minutes later I became aware that he had been staring at me. I braced myself, and sure enough, he spoke up.

"You don't look anything like Harry Potter."

A rough sigh escaped me. I guess it couldn't be helped. "No, I don't."

"You look more like someone on the news a while ago."

"Oh yeah?"

"Yeah, you do."

"What a coincidence." I spat out of my window.

Silence for a few more minutes. There was traffic everywhere, and it was fairly hot outside. We passed a young girl screaming because she had dropped her ice-cream cone while her father, carrying a smaller child, tried to console her.

"What're you doing here?" He asked.

"Going back to college wasn't really an option after that happened." So I openly admitted who I was, for the first time, to someone after the riots. It didn't feel like some release. I was just, as I may have mentioned before, caring less and less about this whole thing. It was tiring and it was greatly annoying to have to constantly be looking over my shoulder. I was getting exhausted and lazy, angry that people wouldn't forget and leave me alone. And sure enough, the young man's eyes opened wide.

"It *is* you."

"Yeah, it's me."

"I-it-what" he stuttered, "what are you doing here? Plumbing?"

"Trying to start over. Turn a new leaf."

"But you, you started the riot. You tried to start a rev –"

"No, I didn't. Those are lies. There were people around me who wanted to, but I was just there."

He tried to formulate his next question as best he could, but only came out with "So how did it happen? Why were you there?"

"Tried to figure that out myself. But then I got tired of thinking about it. And now I'm here, shrugging off people like yourself who are just *so* fascinated with the whole thing."

Undeterred, he continued to prod. "What happened to the others? That girl Elizabeth, an' an' you know…" he looked down, and leaned in a bit. "Dead Richard," he whispered.

"No idea. Heard Richard was dead."

"*Dead?*" He swore under his breath, and the brevity of the word sounded silly against his adolescent tongue. This apparently hit him hard, and he repeated it several times to himself in shock.

"Dead. Wow."

A few more seconds of blessed silence. Hoping his appetite was sated.

"I've read those transcripts, you know." He piped up.

"Transcripts?"

"Of your speech. The one before the riot broke out."

That there were transcripts of that was news to me, and disconcerting. "What - And where are these?"

"Online. People share 'em, talk about 'em."

"I was forced to give those."

"But you did write them, right?"

"I didn't write anything."

He just stared at me. I could feel his eyes searching for some hint of whether or not I was telling the truth. Why I was revealing all of this to this young man was beyond me, and extremely careless to be sure, but I was numb to the whole thing. He didn't say a word for the rest of the ride.

We eventually got to the park, and as he opened the door, I remembered something and called out to him.

"Your father doesn't know who I am, right?"

"He has no idea."

"Good. Look, I would appreciate it if you kept this – "

"Oh, I will." He smiled. The resemblance to Don was already uncanny at his age – bright eyes, ridiculous, mischievous look. As he closed the door, I heard him give farewell.

"Thanks for the lift, Fortunato."

On my drive home, on a whim, I stopped by a gas station and picked up a packet of cigarettes and a lighter. I think I wanted to pick up a bad habit or two, to make things more interesting. Maybe I was bored. I got to my apartment and, setting up on my balcony, got halfway through my first cigarette when I began to cough viciously. My neighbor, an old man with whom I have never been acquainted, was on his balcony, a few feet to the left of mine, and started laughing hard at my plight. I flicked the cigarette over to him, where it landed with a splash of sparks at his slippers. He stopped laughing. We both sat there for a while, watching the tide and the ships roll by, until I went back inside.

As I walked down the hallway to my bedroom that night, I noticed with sudden clarity how long the passage from my living room to my bed was and fell into a dark place - and was suddenly reminded of my long walk out of prison and the twin chain-link fences on either side of me. How silent and lonesome those movements were, socked feet on dirty carpet. The emptiness of my apartment, the solitude got to me, and as I lay down I began to feel myself unravel.

What had I been doing? Moving from one day into the next, drifting from consciousness to sleep. I had always been content to do just that, to exist. Why? Why couldn't I live like other people, find a passion? Why were my emotions mute and nonexistent – why couldn't I feel anything, even now? What was I? I curled up more and more. But I knew this line of fervent, desperate questioning was pointless: soon enough I would revert back into my old self, and look upon such introspection with embarrassment and disgust. Eventually, I faded into slumber.

Hey!
Gentlemen!
Amateurs
of sacrilege,
crime
and carnage,
have you seen

The next day found me at the usual roost, on the second floor of the bar. Today, there was a customer I had not seen before, sitting next to the Asian girl with the sharp bangs. They were sharing between them a single pair of earbuds, and their heads were close to one another because the cord was short. This newcomer was a young white man in an undershirt, and was fairly pierced – his cheeks had large gages in them, and his nose had silver pellets up and down its bridge. Tattoos were visible on his skin, brightly colored, but of what they depicted I couldn't say. His hair was short and strikingly blonde. I hadn't seen frosted tips since I was in elementary school but this guy must have been convinced he could bring them back into style.

I noticed that the usual couple, Benjamin and Katie, were much quieter and less physically intimate in the presence of this new tenant to the floor. They spoke quietly to one another in their usual spot, and Katie, wearing a tight-fitting exercise tank top and large sunglasses splayed on the top of her head, would occasionally glance over at the electronic producer and her acquaintance with what I gradually realized was haughtiness. I suppose that she assumed they were romantically involved, and perhaps that this romance threatened to overshadow hers and Bens. This would be absurd, but based on what I had seen and experienced from being in their presence so often I would not put it past them to be jealous of nothing.

The producer and her boyfriend/friend paid no attention to the increasingly venomous looks, and continued to collaborate on whatever they were working on in the laptop in front of them.

"No, you need to input this file here. Where did you download it to?"

Asian girl's English was not stellar, but she responded confidently. "In, ah, this file here, where I put all of those, ah, types of things."

"There's your problem. You didn't integrate it right, that's why it's not working when you press play. Try this..." and so on. I saw no indication of a romantic relationship between them. Ben repeatedly, I noticed, would try to pull Katie towards him, or kiss her, which was all declined in order to keep her focus on this unwelcome guest. And by the time I left to go downstairs, he was obviously annoyed by that, and I was moderately disgusted.

It was late at night now, around eleven, and I decided I should pack it up for the day and head home. Tomorrow I had a shift with Don at some old folk's home. As I walked past the bar to the exit, someone called out at me.

"Hey, wait a sec."

I paused, and turned around. It had been my bartender – who I did not speak to on any occasions save for when ordering a drink. She was grinning at me. Two of her bottom teeth were ever so slightly out of place, but it was only barely noticeable. She had long, curly, dirty-blonde hair, high cheekbones, and green eyes. She was as tall as me, and she was wearing a black tank top. Leaning over the bar, she officially acquainted herself with me.

"You drive the blue pickup, right? Parked outside?"

I was a little stunned, but I recovered. "Yes, yeah, why?"

"Go wait for me, I'll be out in a second. My name's Lorelei, by the way." And she disappeared into the back room.

I walked out to my truck and waited in the driver's seat, her name rolling lazily on my tongue. I only now noticed that the upholstery was torn or very worn down in the seats, and that the leather had over time cracked and split with age.

Lorelei. LORE-ah-lye.

I don't know why I waited for her then, and like so many decisions involving the impulses of strangers, in retrospect it was reckless of me to do so. She probably had more knowledge of my movements than anybody else, aside maybe from Don. My bartender, the one other person I interacted with routinely. She, for all I knew, could have been one of those agents that hid away in the shadows, that threw stones into shop windows with little death threats tied to them with red string, or who painted murals honoring nonsense. She had seen more of me, certainly, than anyone else had. Maybe monitored my silence and deduced who I was. But for some reason, I didn't feel like driving away. I think a part of me wanted to see where this went, for better or worse, whether this was a trap or not. And she was very pretty, if I was being *completely* honest.

She burst out of the front door about five minutes later, carrying several plastic bags full of what was clearly liquor from behind the bar. She had put on a hoodie now, and, opening the passenger door, tossed a bag to me.

"Thanks! Now, let's get out of here before Leeroy notices."

"Before who notices what?"

"Just drive," she turned to me again as she fastened herself in, beaming once more a smile that I was beginning to think was less genuine than I had originally thought. "I'll explain on the way."

Lorelei. Laurel-eye.

I drove to my apartment. On the way there, she began to laugh, and couldn't stop for a few minutes, finally simply giggling to herself and staring out of the window.

"Interesting way to tender your resignation." She glanced over at me.

"Well aren't you sharp?"

"You don't have a car of your own?"

"Nope," she began looking through the bags and assessing her spoils. "Take the bus usually. But I thought, hey, here's a regular. He'll do."

"I'll do for what?"

"Where are you taking me, stud?"

"My apartment."

"So *forward*!"

"No, it - I'd be more than happy to drop you and your..." I ventured a glance past the plastic folds of one of her treasures. "...*beer* off at the BART."

"No need to get touchy. I like my men brash. And this is more than mere beer, please," she shook a bag indignantly, jingling the glass inside. "All manner of liquor for your pleasure."

We passed under an orange streetlamp, stopping at a red light a few blocks away from my home. It was beginning to drizzle, making pinprick drops on the hood and windshield.

"What's your name, by the way?" She asked me.

"Never picked it up?"

"Not like you really talk to anyone, you know. Just sit there and sulk with your drink."

I gave her another false one. "Why did you just steal all of that?"

"I'm surprised you didn't just drive away, actually."

"I am a little bit, too," She laughed again, and this time it sounded real. "I like you." But she hadn't answered my question yet.

We entered my apartment at around a quarter to midnight, and immediately she cleared off my dining table and laid out all of her loot, commenting on the drabness of my living space.

"No posters or anything? People'd think you were a serial killer. And what's with all of these pizza boxes? Chinese food? Are you a recluse?" She spun around to face me. "You aren't a serial killer, right?"

"How long do you plan on staying here, exactly?" I tossed my jacket onto the couch and looked over her shoulder as she unpacked her bottles.

"Oh, lighten up. Here, have a drink, on me." She tossed me some nondescript can, not once looking up from her unpacking. I sullenly opened it.

By the time she had finished, and thrown the plastic bags into a corner, I realized just how much Lorelei had stolen, and how much a lot of it was worth. All manner of spirits had lain hidden away in the confines of the bar, it seemed – dozens of bottles of whiskey, rum, tequila, scotch and even some wines and coffee liquors had been lifted by my newfound companion's delicate fingers in a manner of minutes. I recognized some more expensive brands and calculated their going rate at liquor stores, trying to tally it all up. My entire table was covered inch to inch with craft beers and the aforementioned fine alcohols, and as if having undergone great strain in laying out her prizes, the thief let out a great sigh and fell into my couch in front of the television.

"That's that. What a haul."

"Still haven't told me why you decided to quit. Is this going to come back to haunt me?" I gazed over the enormous trove and wondered if this could implicate me as an accomplice to robbery.

"It won't. Leeroy loves me too much. He'll be annoyed, but he won't come after me."

"I feel like stealing hundreds of dollars' worth of alcohol should amount to more than irritation." I sat down next to her. She had kicked off her shoes and was arching her back in a feline-like stretch. Her coat now lay atop mine on one of the arms of the couch.

"Then you haven't met Leeroy." She said, surveying my room with a growing sneer on her face. "Bring some of it here, would you? The wine. I love chardonnay. And help yourself."

I watched her for a moment, then decidedly got up and complied, grabbing the corkscrew I had stashed away somewhere in my kitchen, and a drink for me as well. She moved her legs for me to sit next to her on the couch, but as I sat down, she laid them across my lap.

She looked over to the table adjacent to where her head lay, and picked up some small paperback book. *The Wind in the Willows*. I had never read it. I think I had picked it up from my grandmother's place as I was moving out, her wanting to be rid of some of her things and saying I should take a few of her books with me to my new apartment. It was dusty and well-worn, and clearly had been read dozens of times before I had placed it absentmindedly onto the coffee table. On its cover was a nice scene of a river flowing in the English backwoods. I had no knowledge of the characters or the story.

Lorelei tossed the book to me, uncorking her wine at the same time. "Will you read this out loud?"

"What?"

"Read that to me. From the beginning?"

"You want me to read a book to you?" She gave me a reproachful look.

"I like it when people read to me. More intimate than watching the T.V." She looked over at her reflection in the black screen of my television across the room. We made up some sort of inky-black portrait in the frame – her head laid on the arm of the couch, legs over my lap, wine bottle lazy in her hand. And me, somewhat uncomfortable, grasping the novel and trying to avoid touching her ankles.

"Fine," I said, hoping that maybe she would either fall asleep or get bored. Then maybe she'd leave. What in the world was I doing? "Fine. I'll read to you." She smiled wide again, and I realized that the more she smiled at me the more trouble I had distinguishing whether or not she was being fictitious. I put this thought out of my mind and began to recite the tale of the mole and his spring cleaning.

Pages turned to chapters, and the wine slowly disappeared and cans of beer multiplied on my dirty carpet. My words began to slur out and butcher this children's tale of the importance of camaraderie, and Lorelei began to have trouble keeping her head up. About an hour into the book, she sat up straight and, pulling me by my shirt, kissed me mid-sentence just as the Toad had given up boating for racecars. We were both very drunk at this point, and it took me a moment to realize what was happening. The next thing I remember was this ghostly thin visage, now naked, pulling me down the hall towards my bedroom, singing *Whatever Lola Wants*. The innocent little story lay tossed aside on the ground next to two impressive piles of alcoholic beverages, emptied of their nectar.

She was laughing again. She must have immediately guessed that I was a virgin, yet she still pulled me into the dark confines of my room, and we together enveloped one another under the covers of night. Dizzy, nauseous and unfeeling, I let her take me wherever she wished me to go, do whatever she would like, and we fell asleep next to one another at around four AM.

<u>Chapter 8</u>

The light streaming through thin shutters pierced through my eyelids the next morning, and shot a laser directly into my dehydrated brain. I do not usually get hangovers, but this morning was an exception. The unwelcome feeling of spinning while being still did not disappear when I closed my eyes, and the fluttering in my lower abdomen kept me from moving anywhere or any part of my body. I knew what had happened the night before, but couldn't exactly recall whether or not I enjoyed it. It was then that I turned my head to Lorelei – ever so slightly, to avoid the shudders of queasiness – and saw it.

She had fallen asleep on her back, dirty curls spread under her, breasts rising and falling with sleeping breath. Head turned away from the window, so she wasn't facing me. Her left hand was curled up to right under her left ear, and on it beamed a ray of orange morning sunlight, illuminating what I foolishly thought for a moment was an unfortunate birthmark. I squinted.

It was curious, that I had never noticed it before. Not all of those times when she had handed drinks to me at the bar, or when she handed me her bags of stolen goods during her grand robbery. Not when she had taken my hand, in a drunken stupor, and pulled me into dark confines for clumsy, shadowed sex. Only now did I see it: a curious little tattoo. On her left hand, reading from the tip of her thumb to the tip of her forefinger, and crossing the skin in-between, a slogan, in bold, reading **"Cigarettes Are Cool."**

I lay there for a while staring at the thing, hoping maybe that it would go away or disappear, that it was a trick of light in the hot, stuffy little room. Surely there could be no question now – Lorelei must have, without a shadow of a doubt, known who I was. She had seen me, known my identity, and lured me from the safety of being in public. That had to be it.

But for some reason, I didn't want to believe it. Was I wrong? It wouldn't be gloating to say that the riots had received national attention at the time, and that members of the echelon responsible – Dead Richard, Elizabeth and so on – in particular had a lot of coverage diverted to them alone. That little tattoo was Elizabeth's signature mark, to be certain, but could it just have become a fashion statement? Why, if she really did know who I was, why did Lorelei wait until now, after so many months of my patronage, to approach me? Unless – my heart skipped a beat – unless it was a sort of elaborate trap.

I leapt up, greatly daring, and opened my window, fearing to find haphazardly parked cars and students all waiting around my building – but there was no one. A few trucks passed by lazily on the road below. A stray dog, a large Labrador, was sniffing a trashcan near the entrance of the complex. But no one was milling about, searching with excitement the second floor in hopes to see me.

I immediately felt the consequences of moving so quickly and ran to the bathroom, nude, and bent over the toilet. After a few painful minutes I felt better, and shuffled back to the doorframe. She had turned in my bed, but Lorelei had not awoken. After watching her for a moment, I picked my clothes up off of the floor, dressed myself, and went into the kitchen – almost having to run back to the bathroom at the mere sight of all of the booze that remained untouched on the dining room table.

My sickly brain tried to think of some way to remedy or address this situation as I put together some menial breakfast. I really should have just driven off when she asked me to wait for her in the parking lot, and I cursed myself for being so stupid. But there was nothing to be done about it now. What mattered was figuring out Lorelei's intentions, and whether or not she knew who I was (again, almost unquestionable, but I couldn't bring myself to accuse her quite yet). It was entirely possible that she wasn't planning anything, but I could not be sure. But before I could ponder the matter any further, out of my peripherals two arms appeared and embraced me from behind.

"Good morning."

"'Morning," I flipped the egg in my frying pan as she pulled herself from me, not turning to face her. "How are you feeling?"

"A little queasy, but asides from that, okay." I saw out of the corner of my eye that she hadn't bothered to dress. Her hair was a tangled web on her head, and she looked a little pale. She was more hungover than I. "Making breakfast?"

"Yes. Would you like something?"

"I'll make myself some toast."

"Bread's over there," I pointed to a cupboard with the spatula.

We both silently rummaged through the kitchen as we made our separate plates, and then retired to the couch, as the table was still inaccessible. The black frame of the television now showed a disheveled, tired me in drab clothes and a naked young woman next to me, eating lightly and trying not to vomit. I could not bring myself to demand her tell me about that stupid little imprint on her hand, out of fear of awakening in her some recollection of who I was, or of upsetting this delicate balance. I could not be sure that she was plotting something against me, but everything hinged on the origins of the tattoo, and her intentions.

Eventually Lorelei did get dressed, and wordlessly, she left the apartment. I breathed a sigh of relief, hoping that she was gone for good – and yet the image of that tattoo bothered me still. Perhaps she was off to meet with her cohorts, her co-conspirators, to tell them where to find me? I was beginning to regret not pushing where and why she had gotten that tattoo when a few hours later, she reappeared, bags full of potted plants and posters in tow. But without telling me why she had bought these things, she leapt on me, pinning me to the couch, where she proposed, whilst removing her shirt, a repeat of last night. "Only this time we'll remember."

Half an hour later she was asleep on my chest on the couch still, and the black inky portrait beheld us once again. I noticed in its reflection my hand was caressing her head, and, embarrassed, removed it.

"What is all of this?" I demanded when we both recovered, referencing the bags she brought in. She had purchased a cavalcade of lilies, roses, and all manner of flowers in addition to landscape posters of famous paintings.

"I said you look like you live in a serial killer's den, so I decided to spruce the place up for you." She delicately placed a large budding cactus atop my dusty T.V. and then rushed by me to place a glorious purple snapdragon near the entrance to the deck.

"Didn't feel like consulting me before going out and buying all of this?"

"Why would I?" A yellow lily was made the centerpiece of the dining table, pushing away still untouched bottles of wine and ale to make way.

"I didn't ask for any of this." She stopped, and looked at me, surprised.

"I know. Can't I just do something nice?" She asked me seriously. I felt a little guilty for reprimanding her on what seemed to be a truly genuine gesture, but my paranoia had yet to dissipate, and this was all so *incredibly* sudden. We had met formally only yesterday, and had had sex twice in under twenty four hours. Seeing that I was wavering, she perked back up. "Do you have any tape? Help me hang these. You won't even recognize the place when I'm through."

About half an hour later, and we were finished. My home was now a menagerie of colors, tasteless posters, and smelled like a greenhouse. On every surface there were at least two to three different floras, and on every wall hung one or two copies of either a Van Gogh or a Gaugin painting. But just as we finished, I swore loudly – I remembered that I had had a shift with Don today. I quickly ran into the kitchen and called him up. Lorelei looked on with curiosity as I tried to both ask for forgiveness and explain myself over the phone.

"Where were you this morning?"

"I'm so sorry, I completely forgot – did everything go alright?"

"Of course it did, not a huge job. Little lonely, but whatever. You okay? You never miss a shift. And you didn't call in this morning."

"I know – something, something came up, and it totally slipped my mind. Am I going to get into trouble for this?"

I breathed a sigh of relief when Don laughed it off. "No, kiddo, of course not. You have a good record for what time you've been working with us. Take it easy, alright? Everything okay on your end?"

"I, uh, yes. Yes, everything is fine, sorry again. When is my next shift?"

"Day after tomorrow."

"Okay, great. I'll be there. Thanks for understanding." That was too close of a call. This little occurrence with Lorelei almost cost me a job that I happened to enjoy and paid well enough. This mystery had to be addressed, to avoid future complications, to stop myself from worrying so much about it. I had to know what Lorelei was doing here.

I immediately turned to her and finally asked, "What does your tattoo mean?"

She shook her head in confusion. "What? Tattoo – oh, on my hand?" She held it up. "Nothing, really. Just thought it sounded cool."

"Where did you get the idea for it?" I tried to sound as casual as possible.

"Oh, uh, do you remember those riots ages ago? Like some college on the east coast, you remember that?"

"Barely, yeah."

"I didn't follow it much either, but the girl, she was one of the leaders or something I think – she had this tattoo on her hand, and I thought that it was pretty rad."

"'Rad'?"

"Yeah! Got it a few days after the riots ended. Sometimes people will see it and think that maybe I had some part in what happened over there, so I kind of regret getting it. Oh well. Everything okay with your boss?"

"Oh, Don? Yes, we're all squared away. I'm fine."

"Not my fault, is it?"

"Well, kind of." Her face fell here and she looked horrendously guilty, so I quickly tried to spin it around. "Really more my fault for getting drunk last night and not setting an alarm. But I've got a good record with the place, so they let it slide by." This placated her and she turned away, proceeding to pick up the remnants of last night's debauchery. A telltale sign of bottles clinking together told me she was packing all of the empty ones away into one of her empty bags to take away.

Lorelei's explanation seemed plausible enough, and I wanted to believe it. I still couldn't shake the feeling of how my heart had sank at recognizing the tattoo, but she had seemed truthful and innocent enough in her explanation for me to at least, for now, be sated with the matter. Lorelei had yet to prove herself dangerous or conniving. In fact she was only guilty of distracting me from my job and taking my virginity.

The day passed, and that night I found her preparing to sleep in my bed once again. The apartment had been tidied up, decorated, and cleaned, all by her, and yet I couldn't help but ask her if she did not have a place of her own to stay.

"Oh, I do," she replied sheepishly, "on the other side of town. But, you know, I only robbed the bar yesterday. It wouldn't be safe to go back now."

"Using my place as a sort of safe house, then?"

"If that's okay with you."

"Well, I thought you said that...Larry?"

"Leeroy."

"I thought you said that Leeroy wouldn't be too incensed on the stolen alcohol."

"I mean, he'll get over it, sooner than others would. I bet by the end of this week he'll have totally forgotten about it. But right now, I don't know."

End of the week. What was today? I had dropped off Don's suspicious son two days ago, then met Lorelei on Sunday, when she then came home with me. So today was Monday – until around Saturday Lorelei would be using my home as a sort of hideaway until her former employer had given up. But I agreed and said that that was probably a good idea. Then she gave me a huge smile, one as if she was expecting me to fight her on the matter, and leaned over the bed and kissed me. Tuesday, Wednesday, Thursday, Friday, Saturday.

The next few days with Lorelei were not simply a blur – they were wild, intense days fraught with bouts of absurd arguments and sex intermittently. The arguments arose out of nothing and spiraled into topics that reminded me of Don. What were my views on Christianity? Did I feel the need to help other people? How was I growing in my daily life? When my answers to these questions did not satisfy her (and they rarely did), we would argue. She called me soulless, unfeeling and arrogant during the worst ones, and I reminded her, as calmly as I could, that she was in my home hiding from the police, and that she was more than welcome to leave any time. In a way, she reminded me of Elizabeth in a manner that was not altogether flattering. It was these moments that made me seriously reconsider her state of mind.

The day when I was to go to work, I realized that I would need to leave Lorelei alone in my apartment. This made me anxious, but finding no other alternative, I went on my way, leaving her to sleep. The previous night we had had some falling out over literature – she had wanted me to start reading some book on philosophy, but I had absolutely no interest in the matter and put my foot down. Things escalated, and she eventually slammed the door on her way out. She returned to the apartment a few hours later, apologizing, but begging me to at least read one chapter.

Don noticed that my mind seemed preoccupied. While I was usually quiet, I tended to at the very least be focused on screwing or unscrewing something, or reading diagrams, or whatever. Today's work, in a hotel not too far from where I lived, required replacing a recently blown water vein under the foundations. The job was not dissimilar to the very same one wherein Don and I became acquainted, but I was constantly worrying about the state of my home, and what Lorelei might have been doing in it.

"That's the third time you've looked over that pipe, kiddo," Don said. We were in the basement of the building, and with a team of two others. He was right: I had been absentmindedly bolting and re-bolting the same line for the past twenty minutes, while everyone else was doing proper labor.

"Is it?" I asked innocently. "Sorry. I thought I had been working on that line over there."

"Don't worry about that – go grab the replacements from the truck, would you? Should be done in a few hours' time at the most if we stay on task."

"Right, yeah, sure." And I quickly went up the stairs. But I could feel Don's eyes following me, curious.

Eventually the day passed, and while I would usually stop by the bar for a night of eavesdropping, at this point I had envisioned such alarming scenes in my imagination that I sped home immediately to see what Lorelei, in her dementia, had done.

Swinging the door open, I breathed out a sigh of relief: She was sitting on the couch, lunch tray in front of her, reading her book. She looked up at me quizzically, then patted the couch next to her.

That night, as we lay in bed, she asked the ceiling fan a question as it tinged rhythmically and lazily blew the hot air around us.

"Have you ever cried during a movie?"

This caught me by surprise. I had to think about it. I almost told her no, until at the last second I remembered an instance where I did.

"I think so. A long time ago."

She buried her face into my side. The windowpane blinds shuttered quietly as the recycled air and drawn out breath fluttered between them.

"What movie was it?" She asked after a moment.

But it had been too long since. I was a child. "I don't remember."

She turned away to fall asleep after a moment more of silent contemplation, or of waiting for me to ask her the same. The ceiling fan looked down on me as if reproachful. It's ringing became a *tsk-tsk-tsk*. My eyes became heavy and soon closed. I began to think about when the last time I had cried was, and realized that I couldn't remember: even after my grandmother had passed away so recently, the most I had felt was some sort of slight anxiety at how busy the whole situation could have made me. That grief I'd prepared myself for never really came.

The next day was spent largely as the previous ones, with ridiculous conversations and rude comments being tossed side-by-side with almost marital affection.

"You're such a weirdo," she snarled today. "Who doesn't listen to music?" She had recently decided to introduce me to some band she was a fan of, which I did not like. This arose from my lack of any sort of music collection. I guess I should have been nicer letting her down, because when I told her it wasn't really my taste, she became extremely defensive.

"You're more than welcome to go back to Leeroy." She hated that, and she stormed off into my bedroom, slamming the door behind her.

Around lunchtime I brought home a take-out meal, and I came across her writing poetry on the porch overlooking the bay, wearing nothing but a bathrobe I had once bought but never used. She was also smoking the cigarettes I'd bought a few days before, and had accrued at her feet a small pile of cigarette butts. She quickly hid her work away when I walked out to join her.

"Penning sonnets?"

"Ha ha."

"Really, what were you writing?"

She softened when she saw that I wasn't trying to tease her. It was strange. So often her hostility towards me, when it hadn't risen out of ideological nonsense, was because she misread me as being malicious - even our fights were about nothing, so how could I have been expected to hold any sort of grudge? Not once during the time that we had known each other, as short of a time as that may have been, did I intentionally try to hurt her feelings. Why she thought I would ever try to do that, I really never figured out.

"It's...well, I write poems sometimes."

"Can I read one?"

"No!" She was instantly mortified. "No, no no. Never. I...these are for, you know, personal therapy. Do you write anything?" she quickly asked.

"I used to write for this online website. They'd ask for a few pieces a week." It was very nice out today. There was a breeze that smelt of saltwater and flowers from one of my neighbors, who had had the mind to plant a garden of lilacs and roses a few windows down. On a boat a ways down the bay you could make out someone who was playing guitar to a small audience, but what he was playing we couldn't hear.

"What did you write about?"

"All sorts of things. But the publication shut down, so I had to find another job. Hence the plumbing."

"That's terrible. I'd loved to be paid to do what I was passionate about." I resisted the dangerous urge to correct her, and instead reached for my coffee.

"Why don't you? What's your passion?"

"I..." she took a minute to collect her thoughts, and looked over the bay. Her neck glowed in the afternoon sun as she watched the cars glide across the Golden Gate Bridge, so far away, so quiet and distant from herself. So many different people, living different lives, having different struggles or successes we would never understand. We'd never know any of them, and none of them cared to know us. I found that some people had a harder time accepting that than others.

Lorelei, I suspected, was one of those people who had trouble coming to terms with that kind of thing.

"I just want to help people. People who've been hurt." She looked back at me, eyes alight with something in her head. She was being serious. "There's so many people, tossed aside and just forgotten, there's so much hurt in the world, you know? And nobody looks to try to help them."

"Why can't you follow that passion?"

"I have – I am. I'm trying," she deflated a bit, holding her pen and notebook loosely in her lap. "I tried to do psychiatry in college, to get a degree to open my own practice. But that didn't work out for…a few reasons." I didn't push the subject.

"But I just try to help people where I can, now. On the street, sometimes in the bar, when I was there." She piped up, smiling a bit at the reminiscence of past memories that I couldn't see. I can only imagine the repertoire of oddities and strangers that had come and gone in that bar over the years. "In the future I'll have more opportunities to help people I think, but for now, that's okay. I really want to work on prisoner rehabilitation someday." The irony here was not lost on me, but it was likely better not to tell her that I had been in prison recently.

"I think you will," I nodded. "I think you'll do some really amazing things, Lorelei." She looked at me as if she herself didn't believe it, and swallowed hard, glancing away.

She might have just been embarrassed about the poetry, since our conversations hadn't really touched on anything really honest about ourselves up until then. I got up and left, leaving her to her work and her fantasies of altruism. Dreams that we surely must all have, that nobody ever expects to or really wants to achieve.

Every person's life follows a single, beautifully intricate line that makes them wholly unknowable to others. You will never fully understand those around you, simply because you are not them. Whatever seemingly random or thoughtless thing they do is the culmination of all of their lives up to that single point, repeated and evolved, forever. And you must be content with not comprehending, not understanding, or else it will drive you mad.

<u>Chapter 9</u>

The next day I worked once more with Don. I was clearly calmer, now that I was certain that Lorelei wasn't going crazy in my apartment (or at least I was pretty certain). This day we were doing something a bit more exotic, though it was no skunk in a swimming pool. A restaurant perhaps three blocks from where I lived, and one that I occasionally visited, had contracted our firm to update their food disposal maintenance framework, or, in layman's terms, the grease from their grills had caked up so badly in the foundations that a new installation was needed immediately. This entire fiasco was stomach-turning and I swore to never return to the establishment, and embedded a stench in my pores that lasted until I doused myself in three consecutive showers that evening.

Don wasn't so suspicious of me this time around, and by the day's end we'd done our job, although neither of us were all too pleased about it. The sun had set outside and I dutifully waited at the restaurant's meager bar while Don disappeared into the kitchen to harangue the managers. The menus used here were all printed on a thick parchment paper and I noticed, as I dully flipped through one, that the material used was very soft, and that many people had absentmindedly written something atop the menus without realizing that they were leaving a ghost of their notes behind underneath the watermelon green coloring.

"GARAGE SALE AT NOON ON (date incomprehensible)"

"Eggs, milk (?) sour cream, MV, shampoo, sippy cups…"

"Ra-ra-Rasputin, lover of the Russian queen…"

And so on and so forth. I had made it through half of the menus sitting on the bar trying to piece out clues of what patrons had written before, when Don appeared through the kitchen door, brow in a deep V, and his face becoming redder with each passing second. Behind him trailed a chickadee of a man, wearing a blue apron and large full-moon spectacles. He was bald, save for a furry ring of gray hair encircling his scalp, and a great mustache under a small red nose. He was short and plump, and his tiny feet scurried behind the comparatively enormous Don with great pace. I could make out, to my disbelief, that the man was blathering on about the conflict in Kashmir, of all things. At the time I had no idea why or how this subject could have come up, until later on I realized that the man was brilliantly playing to Don's philosophical side by posing the kinds of questions that would have put him on a tangent. They must have been acquainted prior to this.

"Some say that it's the most beautiful place on Earth," he chirped, as he and Don eventually stopped a few feet from me to sit at the bar. "A garden of Eden. Which I think makes the fighting there all the more, dare I say, romantic. Which side do you think has a better claim?"

But Don must've known himself better than I gave him credit, because he wasn't having any of it. "You're an idiot, and the price is fixed at $8,000. Any other firm would have tripled that. And frankly," he whipped around and glared down at the man and said, loud enough for the patrons around him to hear, "I've never seen such a *filthy, poorly run* and *disgusting* establishment in my entire career. You'll - "

"Alright, alright," hissed the manager. His genial mask vanished. "You've always been...fine. Fine." He threw his chubby little hands up, and stalked back into the kitchen, calling back "expect it on Monday."

Don straightened up a bit, a little smugly. His face had quickly returned to its normal, partially jovial resting state and the color was returning.

"Well done," I said, standing up. My knees were exhausted and my arms were aching from the work we'd put in. In the case that this plumbing thing didn't pan out, I made a mental note to never work in the food industry.

"That's Sam for you," he snorted as we made our way outside. A few patrons that had heard Don's remarks were also hastily calling for their checks. "Known him since high school, always been a conniving, cheap ass."

When I returned home I arrived at the sight of Lorelei waiting for me at the bottom of our apartment stairwell. Her face brightened up, and she ran to me as I got out of the car. She flashed a pair of concert tickets.

"I think the reason you didn't like my music was because you haven't seen them play live." She was beaming. "They're actually playing downtown tonight! Show's at seven, and my friends will be there. I can introduce you to them."

This presented a dilemma. I did not want to see this band. I did not want to waste my time in some cheap venue with a group of strangers, dark, sweaty and annoyed after a long day of work. I did not want to be introduced to her friends. However, keeping Lorelei happy enough to sleep with me took precedence. If I did not take what was intended, surely, as a genuine gift, she would be angered beyond belief, and I doubt that I'd make any use of the last few nights of our cohabitation that we had left. The tension between us as of late had been such that there might not have been any coming back if I told her no.

"Sure, why not."

After a shower, which didn't rid me completely of the stench of grease, and a change of clothes, we were off for a hopefully short night. The concert was being held across town, and after weaving through busy streets and some suspicious alleyways aglow in the setting sun, we arrived at a large white building in the middle of a familiar area. It was standing by itself, surrounded by empty, old parking lots. I was not sure how I recalled the abandoned factory warehouses, the cracks on the pavement and the brown, abandoned trees until I realized with a shiver that not two blocks away was the spot where the mural dedicated to the riots had been painted, before I covered it up. Surely there was no correlation, but the coincidence was unsettling. I followed Lorelei, who was skipping, inside. We turned our tickets in to an acne-ridden, clearly annoyed teenager and finally entered the wide open room.

The show had already started. The room had a very high ceiling with cracked windows, and the stage that the band was playing on was questionably secure. There were a good amount of people there, everyone shrouded in the darkness, alight only at brief moments when some show lights would shine or flash. Lorelei took my hand and dragged me to the front row, where she tried to show me off to a faceless mass of individuals. I pretended to hear their names and smiled politely as she rattled off introductions, but I couldn't see anyone and definitely couldn't hear anything. I didn't want to endanger the sex myself and my roommate were likely going to enjoy in a drunken bout of hormones by the night's end. I wanted everything to go well, and sure enough, she was smiling again – from what I could tell.

The frontwoman of this band insisted on referring to herself as Ester Prinn. She repeated this moniker throughout the unimpressive set several times, making sure the audience appreciated her great creativity and obviously vast knowledge of literature. It was for this poisonous attitude that I decided even more firmly that this band, having already been acquainted with their music, was irredeemably terrible, and when a hat started making its way around for donations about a half hour later, I poured the remainder of a warm beer I'd been drinking into it as a small sign of indignation.

This would come later. Right now, Lorelei leaned over to me, and shouted in my ear:

"I saw a bar on the way in on the right, can you get me a drink?" I nodded, and quickly pushed my way to the back of the concert. I was already sweating because of how hot it was in there. People were all dressed up in tanks and jeans, and I saw a few shirts bearing the name of the band. But the girl whose chest I was accidentally staring at sneered at me and turned around, and her boyfriend glared at me, and I went back to buy our beer. The line was thankfully pretty long, and there was only one poor, understaffed bartender there. The less I had to hear of this garbage the better.

For some reason, my mind drifted back to Elizabeth. This was the kind of environment she would have enjoyed, I think. It was wild and loud, and filled with bad ideas just bubbling underneath the surface and crawling like shadows in the back corners near the venue walls, where leery-eyed creeps jostled to themselves and eyed the crowd with a disturbing hunger. I wondered what she was doing now, if she had gone back to finish her degree. Most likely not, if I knew her well at all. I think I remember hearing from someone that her prison sentence, short as it may have been, left a mark on her. But I couldn't remember who told me that.

By the time I was up to order, two songs had been played, but I wasn't paying any attention to them. I slowly made my way back to the crowd, where Lorelei already had a beer in her hand, and she was laughing very hard. She grabbed me and introduced me to another one of her friends, who I could only barely make out to have a nose ring and green-tinted hair, who was appraising me with a judgmental look. She was heavily freckled, and was very sweaty: my guess was that she'd been in here since the band started playing.

While we hadn't been here very long, Lorelei must have drunk very quickly whatever her friends had given her, as she was clearly a few in. "Thiss's Jenna!!" She screamed at me,

"I've known her since…" and she trailed off. Her friend was still glaring at me, past the point of politeness when it came to appraising a new romantic partner in a friend's life. Lorelei suddenly became very distracted by something that was happening on stage, and screamed and rushed forward, leaving us behind. Her friend quickly leaned in.

"You've been fucking her, huh?" She slurred, "Think you're good enough for her?"

"I'm better," I immediately responded. I must have been pretty annoyed. Even if she was just acting like a drunk fool, I didn't like her attitude, and she was a little close.

I didn't expect her to shove me, and I was pushed into a big guy who grunted and shrugged me off. She called me something, but I didn't hear what it was. "If you fucking hurt her – did you, we, she and me, we've fucked, you know? She and I have fucked, she's screamed my name…" She stumbled forward and lurched on the floor, splattering some bystander's shoes, who then screamed and swore loudly. She pulled her hair up, undeterred. One of her eyes had turned lazy. "I bet you can't even make her cum."

This was embarrassing, but one of her friends had heard the commotion after Jenna threw up and took her by the shoulders and rushed her off in the direction of the women's room. I'd had enough by now, and not wanting to deal with any more of Lorelei's friends, I pushed my way to where I had seen her go, the very front of the stage. I was getting stared at by the more sober patrons who had witnessed everything.

I finally reached her. I figured out that she'd had to have taken pills or something, because there was no way alcohol alone would have gotten her this messy in so short a time. But as I reached out to her to grab her shoulder, in a split second, I looked up on the stage.

I recognized someone playing. The guitarist. He was wearing a shirt, the same shirt I had seen him wear when I met him at Santa Cruz, a logo of The Who. Thomas was his name. He was singing, his hair was a wet mop of sweat as he surveyed the crowd. And for a split second, we locked eyes, and suddenly I realized, he knew.

As the light of recognition started to fill his face, in that moment, something clicked. This man had met me and he undoubtedly knew who I was. And sure enough, his face turned to me, and his mouth twisted in the form of a shout, his eyes widened – an alarm to the concert-goers, that I was here. But by the time that he had interrupted his own lyrics and said something in his microphone, I had torn Lorelei from the crowd and burst out onto the street faster than I thought I could run.

I fumbled with my keys and finally opened the truck as a couple of people began to run out after us. We hadn't parked far, but dragging Lorelei was slowing us down. Someone shouted something and I heard voices closing in on me as I threw her into the passenger seat, shoved my keys into the ignition, and sped off. In the rearview mirror my eyes were red and my forehead was dripping with sweat, but the parking lot was shrinking, and the small crowd in it had stopped running.

"Mmmm..." Lorelei moaned at my right. I glanced at her. She was sucking on her fingers and looking at me, stretching and wiping the hair out of her eyes. She was completely, utterly oblivious to anything that was going on.

I meandered through side roads and alleyways, until I finally reached my apartment. I quickly brought Lorelei inside and returned with a large tarp that Don had left behind after one commission or another. I parked the truck under a tree at the far end of the parking lot, covered it to the best of my abilities, and ran back inside.

Lorelei was sprawled on the bed, moaning and running her fingers through her hair. What she had taken I had no idea, but I was planted near the window, looking through the blinds. I ignored her as she called out to me, begging me in a messy tone to come to bed. Eventually I heard soft snores.

Around half an hour later, I noticed a line of cars drive by on the road. The last one in line turned and drove slowly through the lot, inspecting – whoever was driving as well as the passenger was shining a flashlight onto the cars they drive past. They came to my truck and stopped. The flashlight waved over the tarp for a few moments – then, I heard voices, and the car turned around and drove off.

I waited only a few minutes more. Outside it was dark, and seeing no return of any vehicles, I finally turned around to see Lorelei asleep. A small pool of spit had accumulated near her mouth. Exhausted, and no less worried, lay down next to her and tried to rest. I tossed and turned for a few moments, but I couldn't relax.

I got up and wandered into the living room. It was a mess, but less of one than it usually was. Still a respectable pile of beer bottles and wine on the dining table, but at least the pizza boxes and Chinese food had been disposed of. The outline of the posters Lorelei had bought me were dark on the wall, and appeared like window frames into an inky, black abyss. The plants she bought had been neglected almost immediately, and while I couldn't see their color, I knew they were browning. I lay down on the couch, but I noticed on the coffee table the book I had read to Lorelei the day she effectively moved in. I turned on the lamp and opened it, resuming where I had left off. Half an hour later, I felt a little better and went back to bed.

The next morning I awoke to thunder shaking the windows, and rain smacking the glass hard. I was still very tired, so it must have been very early. I turned over and saw Lorelei sitting on the side of the bed, her head in her hands. I figured whatever she had taken the night before must have given her a pretty bad headache, but hearing me move, she suddenly sat up and turned around, and flashed me that unconvincing smile. Lightning flashed and illuminated her better for a fraction of a second, and I was surprised to see that her eyes were red and her face was a little wet.

"Hi."

"Hi. How did you sleep?"

"Not great," she lay back down, not taking her eyes off of me. "You?"

"I'm still a little tired." We both watched the ceiling fan for a bit.

"Hey, I want to go to the beach. There's a nice spot near the Cliff House."

"Okay."

"I want to go today." I looked at her, trying to gauge her.

I looked out the window, and back at her. "Do you."

"Please?" She looked directly at me. "Please take me there?"

Normally I would be annoyed, and I still was a little bit, but for some reason there was an urgency in her voice that I couldn't place, so I decided to placate her.

"Sure." She jumped up. I slowly pulled myself out of bed.

We were on the road maybe ten minutes later. She insisted on going to the beach during the storm, not waiting for it to pass, for what reason I could not imagine. She was far quieter than usual, and had none of that scathing, predictable wit to throw at me. I fully expected a questionnaire of what I thought of her favorite band, having seen them live, or how the rest of the night went which she couldn't remember. Or even what I thought of her friends. But she was silent.

The rain had let up, thankfully, and I mentioned to Lorelei that we were fortunate. She shook her head.

The Cliff House was an expensive diner atop a scenic cliff next to a large beach, backed by tiny pastel houses which went for millions. From what I understand it was once reminiscent of a castle – I had seen pictures - and was a fantastic nightclub sometime in the early 1900's. But it burned down, and was replaced with a small little box built to make money, not memories. We parked near it and walked down the sidewalk leading to the beach. We were completely alone, and both of us were happy about that. The weather drove off all activity. Maybe that's why she wanted to go during the storm.

When we passed the small stone fence separating the sand from the concrete, Lorelei took off her shoes, placed them against the wall, and began skipping around. Her mood was improving by the moment. The rain was still falling, but it wasn't horrible. The clouds, however, were still very dark, a churning gray and almost black palate which indicated an incoming repeat thunderstorm.

I walked up closer to the beach's edge, where the water kissed it rhythmically. I hadn't been to a beach since Santa Fe, and it felt good to be back at one. Behind me I heard her running back and forth and doing cartwheels. Far, far off in the distance white streaks struck the ocean with a distant clap which arrived seconds later, illuminating the black clouds and casting faraway shadows. Off to my right, atop the stoic beach house, seagulls were screeching and flapping against the incoming winds. Below, against the rocks, waves of greater and greater size exploded into white foam and shuddering roars. I took a deep breath: maybe Lorelei had been right to go to the beach in this type of weather.

Suddenly, she practically tackled me from behind in a hug. She ran off, giggling, and I brushed myself off.

She was facing the ocean, and the rain was falling harder. Her hair was whipping up faster and faster into a frantic wave of blonde curls. Her ankles and forearms were covered in sand. I only now realized that she didn't bring a coat, and was wearing shorts. She must have been freezing.

"We should probably be heading home soon," I called out after a bit. The rain was pelting us now, and hit the sand like small bombs, leaving tiny soaked craters all around our feet. She hadn't heard me, so I put my hand on her shoulder.

She turned to me in complete surprise, as if having forgotten that I was there. Her face was completely wet. But so was mine.

She regained her composure, smiled, and took my hands in hers. "Isn't this the best beach weather?"

"I'm glad we came out here today," I answered. She laughed.

The thunderstorm had moved in, and the ocean's current swelled and crashed over her shoulder. She kissed me on the cheek, and let go of my hands, and turned back around. Her clothes tore at her frame wildly with the wind, as if trying to fly off of her or take her away somewhere.

"Do you know who I am?" I heard myself ask aloud, over the roaring ocean. For some reason I felt like something was happening here. Between us. I couldn't put my finger on it, but my gut told me that now was as good a time as any.

She looked back and raised her eyebrows. A single strand of hair had glued itself to her forehead, and when her eyebrows rose it pushed the hair up to make a sort of upside down "U".

"No," She said, "Who cares who you are?"

She kissed me one more time then, on the lips. Then she turned back around and, taking a deep breath, skipped towards the ocean, dancing. She jumped and sauntered until she was up to her waist, and swam out, fully clothed, further and further away, over and under rising bulbs of seawater.

She soon became a small black dot ravaged by the unrelenting current, pulled and tossed by the sea. Through the rain I could only barely make her out as on her left flank a large wave overtook her, and she disappeared completely.

It dawned on me that she was trying to drown herself. To my credit I acted faster than I thought I would in a situation like that, though not exactly with grace. I swore to myself and hastily pulled out my phone, then dropped it in the sand, then quickly picked it up and dialed 9-1-1.

"9-1-1, what's your -"

I was panicking and speaking hastily, but I was clear. "I'm at Ocean Beach, near the Cliff House. My friend is drowning and there's no lifeguard on duty."

The dispatcher paused. Then, absurdly,

"In this weather?"

"I'm going after her. Send someone over here."

I dropped the phone just as he told me not to do it, quickly took off my shoes, and dashed into the tide. To call it "frigid" is not sufficient enough - the Pacific ocean is cold enough as is, but in the storm it was glacial. I was saved from going into shock by adrenaline alone, the water jolting me alive and turning every pore on my body to ice as I plunged in and swam out against the current.

The waves became massive and overbearing by the time I had pushed myself out to where I thought I had seen Lorelei vanish. Instead of having a view in each direction of the water, the sea rose and fell in great, thundering hills that turned and crashed with the wind. I screamed out her name, fearing that she was gone, and that soon I might be as well.

I suddenly caught a glimpse of her hair and head barely atop a wave building up on my right, and on the verge of descending again. Her eyes were closed, peaceful, but as I reached through the water and frantically grabbed at her they shot open with indignation and surprise.

I pulled at her, with what waning strength I had left, but I felt her rip free from my grip. I think she wanted to shout something at me, but we were both so frozen that our teeth chattered and our lips were blue. She turned and stiffly tried to swim away, just as lights flickered in the storm and through the water and briefly illuminated us both from behind. Two lifeguards on rescue boards had found us, and were shouting something that we couldn't make out. I saw her turn back at me, her face a mix of horror, fury and despair, then, in an instant, it was none of those. She surrendered, and the both of us were brought back to the shore.

The storm had seen fit to begin to subside only when we were back on land, so the rain was letting up and the sky had begun to lighten. The paramedics had thrown some towels on us and were taking a statement from me. I'm not sure how much use I was to them.

"What exactly happened?"

"S-she t-tried to drown her-herself."

They tried to get me to join them in the ambulance, and I was about to get in when I looked at Lorelei. She was sitting next to another paramedic, who was speaking to her, but she was glaring straight at me. Draped in a thin towel, shaking.

If I close my eyes even now I can see her face as if it were a framed portrait, hung up on a wall somewhere to stare down at me as some form of punishment. I don't think I'll forget it, ever.

She was giving me such a contemptuous, dark look through her curled, frozen-solid bangs that it stopped me as I had one foot up on the ledge. It took my breath away, the anger, the hatred that she now suddenly found, eyes burning black in a face turned white and drained of blood for the frigid cold. In all the time that I knew her, this one moment was the most honest she had ever been. And it was a moment of pure, undisguised malice, like the good moments we had shared had never happened, and that I was some sort of stranger who had horribly hurt her in some wordless, careless fashion.

She just glowered at me, too full of hate to actually spew any of it at me. That to release any small fraction of it built up in her might cause her to simply erupt.

I almost fell backwards, trying to tear my eyes from hers. Red with saltwater but still somehow beautifully green.

"No, no," I mumbled to the EMT's. One tried to help me back in, but I was myself beginning to feel some outrage flaming up in me. "I'm fine."

I looked back into the ambulance, but Lorelei's head was hanging down in resignation. "I'm going home," I said to no one in particular, and turned to stumble back towards my car, blood turned to ice but my head full of fire. Eventually I heard the ambulance doors shut, as if hesitant to do so without me, and speed away. I was completely alone on the beach.

Water still dripped from my hands, white with cold, down onto the muddy sand, and snot flowed from my nose freely, dribbling over my lips and mixing with the salt and wet with every step. As I reached the sidewalk, I passed Lorelei's shoes. I considered bringing them with me, and then decided against it. They were soaked through and filthy anyways.

And as I drove off I knew that I wasn't going to see her again.

<u>Chapter 10</u>

When I got home it was still raining out. The first thing I saw was one of Lorelei's posters on the wall, and then, looking around, the brown plants. I picked up one of the bottles of wine we had left and sat down on the couch. The T.V. reflected me, alone, in its black frame as I uncorked the pinot noir and had a few swigs. I sat there and drank for at least an hour until I began to feel my head spin, and then I took special notice of the plant atop of the T.V. It was leafy and big, and it draped over the sides in neglect. It was assuredly dead.

I looked back around the room. Dead plants and posters of art peeling off of the walls. Bottles toppled over.

I remember my throat closing in a restrained cough - whether of some fever coming on or out of bubbling resentment I couldn't say - as I recounted the events of the days prior. Going over details – me bringing her home, her getting me drunk…fighting, making small talk about nothing, her apologizing and trying to encourage some meaningful conversation…introducing me to her favorite band. Reading to her. *The Wind in the Willows* was still on the table, earmarked from where I had left off the night before. This had all been a ploy. She had been planning something along these lines since the day we met.

Lorelei had sought to infect me with affection. Small tokens of her ghost and constantly being around her were meant to make me fall in love, to be utterly destroyed at her suicide. She would walk around the apartment naked, showing off her youthful body. She had desperately tried to infatuate me, to find some common ground to cement herself onto, by being so, so…

I stumbled into my bedroom and had my suspicions confirmed when I saw a small, folded up note on my pillow. She must have written it and left it there while I was getting ready in the morning. I did not open it. I took it, ripped it up, and washed it down the sink. I felt no anger. I was not mad, or even grievous. Had I known what she had planned to do, surely I would have tried to talk to her, stop it before the last second– or so I told myself. I couldn't be sure that I wouldn't have simply disregarded her altogether and removed her from my life to rid myself of the trouble.

No, instead I felt pity that she chose me, of all people, to make this last great effort on. Had she chosen anyone else, I'm sure, with her beauty and little quirks, somebody else would still be at that beach, sobbing and completely traumatized. But I saw through her. And I refused to be used.

The plants and posters were all in the dumpster behind the apartment an hour later, and I was sitting in front of the T.V. watching the news, on my second bottle of wine. I resolved to rid my memory of her completely, by drinking myself into oblivion, and condemning those past days with her to nothingness. I could feel something unfamiliar and red growing in my chest, and I wanted to drown it away. This was unrealistic, but I still tried.

That night, I had fallen to the floor and not gotten up. I only vaguely remember the news on the sideways television, and a story of how many accidents had occurred in the terrible weather. The reporter was at Ocean Beach, filming the recession of the black clouds. In the background, behind her, I saw a small, furry head appear in the waters, then dive back down.

I will die alone, I remember thinking to myself, shag carpet barely perceptible against my numb face; I will die alone, unloving and unloved, and completely, utterly free.

I resolved to drink Lorelei out of my mind. To black out the memory of her via alcohol. I forced beer down my throat at first, then liquor, the first thing the next day when I awoke. By late morning I was drunk. The hours would lull into one another, and aside from using the bathroom, getting alcohol (or water – I knew the dangers of alcohol poisoning, but I wasn't going to let that put an end to my endeavors) or food, I remained seated on the floor, trying to watch television through blurred eyes. Everything constantly spun. My tongue became saturated with the dry taste of whisky and rum, my entire body lost feeling. At one point I had to make a conscious effort to keep my mouth from being mindlessly agape. But I could still see her face in my mind, so I continued to drink and drink. Soon, I completely blacked out. However, in my unconsciousness, I continued to consume – there would be small bouts where I would regain awareness and find new bottles and cans strewn about me, and vomit dried on my shirt. My arms and knees would soon begin to bruise and ache, because in my state I was banging into and bumping around almost every obstacle in my path when I would try to make the journey to either the kitchen or the bathroom.

My veins flowed brown with bourbon, green with absinthe, and white with wine. Part of me began to fear that even though I was including water and food in my diet, I would succumb. That was very frightening, not because of the prospect of death itself, but because the unknowing onlooker may then see my corpse and incorrectly think that this was a lover's suicide out of grief. This was unacceptable, and at the end of the third day of this binge, I threw myself onto my bed, and admitted defeat. Lorelei still swayed and flowed in the cauldron of my memory – but her vision was cracked, and small details had been expelled or blotted by my actions. In a way, I had my victory, to some small degree.

The next day I awoke with a start to see Don sitting at the end of my bed, with a terribly worried expression on his face. He was dressed in his work uniform, and had been shaking my foot. I tried to speak, but my head was in the worst pain I had ever experienced. With every passing second it worsened. When he spoke, I wished desperately to tell him to be quiet – every minor action or sound movement sent spasms through my skull.

"I saw the bottles on the floor. I thought you were dead, kid – I've been calling you since yesterday. You've missed two shifts. Jesus, I was about to call the hospital."

I made a small groaning sound to indicate my discomfort, and Don thankfully understood, nodding sagely.

"You're probably experiencing the worst hangover in the world, I bet. I'll get you some water or something."

So worried was Don for my wellbeing that he called off work and stayed at the apartment for the rest of the day. He explained away my absence from plumbing and vouched for me.

I did not move an inch. I had missed work for the past two days and had not said a word to anyone. We had had several maintenance jobs, one in a school and one private contract from an upscale apartment complex that the firm had been preparing for, and I was not present at either occasion. Don brought me what food I could stomach, and when the sun had set I was almost at least partially recovered.

Don was sitting in a chair in the corner of the room now, leaning forward with his elbows on his knees, and still wide-eyed with concern. When he saw that I might be feeling a bit better, he quietly asked, no fanfare or fluff. "Tell me what happened, kid."

It all flowed out of me, slurred and exhausted. My entire body ached. I didn't make an effort to hide anything, even the sex, except for why we left the concert so quickly the night before she tried to kill herself. From the very beginning, Don heard it all: how she stole all of her liquor, how we got piss drunk. Staying with me for days, walking around naked, writing poetry and calling me a freak, a loser. Our nonsensical, ridiculous fights. The night at the venue. The next day, at the beach. Drinking.

By the end of it I was even more tired due to the monumental effort I had given to relate all of this, but Don had turned gray. The color had left his face. He hadn't moved an inch unless it was to cover his mouth in some contemplative thought.

He whispered something behind his huge, gnarled hand. He looked back at me, and in the darkness I couldn't tell if his eyes betrayed some kind of fear or sympathy.

Don asked if he could stay a little longer – he seemed very worried about me, more so now that he knew the cause of all of this – but I stoutly refused. I was embarrassed that he had taken so much time off as he had for my sake, and humiliated that my retort to Lorelei's trickery had only resulted in me being in tremendous pain. I insisted that all I needed was a day or two to recover, and that I would call him when I was prepared to work again. I didn't forget to thank him as he was leaving, but he just shook his head and closed the door.

That night I did not dream of Lorelei, and I woke up relieved. I was determined to put her out of my mind for good.

I was true to my word and called Don a few days later, after I was sure that I was physically alright. He still had some worry in him, but I was stern, and I joined him on a job later that day. He did not ask any more questions, and with his silence I knew that the whole affair could officially be put to rest, at least for the time being.

I realized that I had not been to the bar in a while, and decided that the quickest route to normality was resuming my previous routine. After work I drove on up to it, but as I got out, from a distance I saw old Eddie wheeling himself in, with his rotting catch on his lap. I walked up to the door, and just as I reached to open it out he burst, eyes red and teeth gnashing in sudden, unexpected pain. He was crying, in grief, tears making dark gray dots on his filthy shirt. He choked and sobbed, and wiped his eyes with his sleeve, and as he rolled away in a fit of despair he did not notice his fish fall off of his lap and smack onto on the sidewalk. I saw the heat of the catch radiate in the afternoon sun, and when I would leave the bar later, the fish would be gone. Taken by some rodents or seagulls, but a yellow stain would remain on the pavement until the rains came again. That was the last time Eddie appeared at the bar, to my knowledge. I straightened my jacket and walked inside to meet Leeroy and get these painful introductions over with.

The jukebox was actually playing music today. The lyrics became clearer as I approached the bar and the inattentive, rude bartender.

"...I've never done good things,
"I've never done bad things,
I never did anything out of the blue..."

He was a lanky younger man a few years older than me with a long, bushy, black beard, bald head and round, thick glasses. He stood about a foot and a half above me, and, hearing the door shut as I walked in, stopped rubbing his temples and gazed in my direction. He offered no friendly greeting, no acknowledgement of me, and went on wiping down the counter. I walked up to him and asked for a beer. He paused, gave me a barely withheld glare, and took his time getting it for me.

"$4.00".

I started. His voice was the one reciting all of the poetry on the jukebox. In my surprise I didn't take the beer or put down any money. He got impatient with the four seconds that it took for me to register who he was, and, dropping the rag and slapping his palms on the bar, looked me square in the eyes.

"Something the matter?"

"You must be Leeroy." I finally found my voice.

"Yes."

"You... I hear your voice on the jukebox sometimes." This invited no response, and his standoffish pose did not loosen up. I tried again.

"Where's the old bartender?"

"Gone."

"I'm sorry to hear that. She was...popular, around here."

"She was."

"Did she work here long?"

A pause as he swallowed something down. I regretted pushing him on it. "$4.00, sir."

I paid. There was nobody else on the first floor, but as rude as Leeroy may have been, the Asian girl was still in her spot upstairs. For the first time she and I acknowledged one another as I climbed up, sharing a friendly nod and smile and recognizing that, while some things had changed here, this was still our bar.

Admittedly, Leeroy's new role as bartender changed the dynamic of the place. It was as if Lorelei was the piece that had held it all together. Or, perhaps that isn't appropriate. She was not some divine thing we all flocked to. Rather it was like a precarious balance had finally broken. As time went on, I would see the effects of this. But for now, at least, while a crisis had happened, things were still intact. This was a bad spot, but the bar would rebound.

Nobody else came to the bar that day. As I was leaving later, I walked downstairs just as the jukebox was being used to play what I thought was poetry for the first time that day. Leeroy was sitting across from it, several empty bottles in front of him. He had put a few quarters in, and a track was starting up. It started out as a dialogue between Leeroy and Lorelei. I stood at the bottom of the stairs and listened.

"Come on, Lore..."

"Get away from me with that mic."

"Come on! It'll be fun. Sing for me. Sing for the customers."

Laughter. "Are you drunk?"

"You've got a *beautiful* voice." The sound of something being moved around, and a scratch as a needle is dropped onto a record. Some soundtrack began to play, and Lorelei groaned.

"You're so embarrassing, turn this off."

"If you're not gonna sing I will." Leeroy, perched like a statue now, puts his face in his hands.

"*Whatever Looola wants*, bum ba bum - "

"*Loooola gets.*"

"There it is! Beautiful."

More laughter, then she's singing. "*And little man, little Lola wants you...*" Leeroy drinks. I take my leave. At this point the wind is blowing fiercely, and I'm reminded of the first time I came here.

It would be disingenuous to say that Lorelei did not affect me in some lasting manner, albeit in a way she certainly did not intend. I desired now more and more what I had had a taste of. A voracity for sex arose in me with each passing day - San Francisco girls in shorts and thin, loose shirts were suddenly a lot more noticeable to me at the beaches, bars, sidewalks. I know that women, as they grow older, become attuned to an inane ability to feel the eyes of men crawling over them, desiring them. Some felt this from me and gloated in it – slouching in one way, stretching, putting up or letting down their hair. More, maybe more mature, ignored it. And a few, more modest or perhaps just completely disinterested, tried in vain to hide their discomfort. Regardless, my abdomen tightened and I grew uncomfortable with every attractive girl I passed, like I was experiencing puberty for the first time all over again. But as time went on, the more and more this happened, the less self-conscious I felt about it. It wasn't like I was the only sexual creature in the world. I was convinced that this was normal, and that surely women experienced the same longing. I tried to bury this newfound sensation with embarrassment.

I wish I could say that this was the only consequence of our relationship, but once more I had trouble sleeping. In fact, I was consistently waking up in the middle of the night for the week after, and one day when Don called me to check in, I complained to him out of frustration and insomnia.

"Haven't been sleeping too well lately."

"Well, figures. I've got some pills that'll knock you right out. Next time we work together I'll bring 'em."

"I appreciate it, but I'll just go to the pharmacy."

"And blow like $30? No, take my stuff. You'll sleep like a rock."

I decided to take him up on his offer, thinking that it would be nothing more than something you could buy over the counter. But when we worked together a few days later, mending some bathroom in a local elementary school, he handed me a clear orange plastic pill bottle with no labelling, almost crushed in the mountainous callouses of his hand.

There had been some lead found in the water of the school, and we were called in to try and find out as discreetly as possible what the problem was. I turned the pill bottle over in my hand as he went back underneath the sink to finish unscrewing something. The lights above us were old and yellow, and barely illuminated the bathroom tiles, but the shadows under the fat rolls on his neck were still clear. "What is this?"

"I had knee surgery a while back and they gave me this to help me sleep through the pain. It'll knock you out."

"Is this safe?" The pills were huge and black. There were six of them.

"What? Yeah, of course. Take one before you go to sleep."

Some children peeked at us from behind the door, giggling. Before we had made it to the bathrooms we had been ogled and jeered at by some kids down the hallways. One, very blonde, shouted that Don looked like a clown, only to be reprimanded by their teacher.

"Why are these jumpsuits so colorful, anyway?" I asked. I never wore one, only being part-time, but all of Don's associates and full-time plumbers resembled the full spectrum. I had even seen one wearing magenta.

"I don't know. Think it's s'posed to make us stand out from other plumbing companies."

Painted on the walls around us were cartoon fish with word bubbles saying "wash your fins!" and "don't forget to flush!" Paint was chipping off of them though and in some places you could see the sickly pale wall underneath. I tucked the pills away and brought them home.

It was raining and windy outside again when I took my first dosage. Sometimes a palm tree near the window above my TV would creak and snap if the weather was bad enough, and the leaves would scrape the glass, and I remember my lights flickering dubiously as I unscrewed the cap. True to his word, about ten minutes after I swallowed one pill, I only barely made it to my bed before completely losing consciousness. That night I got an excellent sleep.

From here on out, something very strange began to happen, for which I have never found a decent explanation. Don later hypothesized that it was due to some alcohol still being left over in my system from the outrageous bender I had gone on, and swore that he had never experienced what I would after starting to take those pills. I still don't know where they came from, or what they contained. After this first night, I began to lapse in and out of consciousness while still being fully awake, over a period of several days.

It started the next day. I had it off, so I figured that I would go to the bar. The jukebox was being particularly somber that day, with Leeroy's voice crooning off in poetic bravado.

It was still largely empty, but the three students had made it back to their roost on the first floor, and were talking in impassioned voices about a bizarre test of strength. Louis and Walker were both admonishing George for what sounded like a matter of absurd pride.

"You couldn't tackle a horse," Louis said, shaking his head. "You couldn't do it. They're massive, they bite and they got hooves. It would hurt and probably kill you. It would at least break a bone or two."

George looked genuinely upset - not angry, but hurt that his friends thought he couldn't tackle a horse. "Do you both seriously think I couldn't? I would wrap my arms around its head and drag it to the ground. It would be over in like five minutes tops."

Walker was uncharacteristically fuming. He threw up

his hands. "First it was a bear. Then a *gorilla*. What is the matter with you? If it is a wild animal it should be considered completely insane. Anything that lives outside should be considered dangerous and past human reckoning."

"You're just saying that because you couldn't fight any animals," George sniffed, looking his small friend up and down. "Survival of the fittest and you're the bottom of the totem pole. The only reason you haven't succumbed to a stray dog or something is because you've got no meat on your bones."

Walker scratched his cheek and considered this for a second. His friends both watched him, waiting for some kind of rebuttal.

"Well," he finally said, "I could probably take on most fish if we were on dry land. Most."

I could almost hear Louis' eyebrows shoot up. "What the hell do you mean 'most'?"

Leeroy was sitting in a chair behind the bar, still looking plenty morose, didn't even acknowledge my entrance, and almost hit me with the glass when I asked for an iced tea.

Upstairs, Ben and Katie were in each other's arms, whispering nauseatingly sweet promises to each other, and the Asian girl, who I was beginning to suspect might've actually lived here, was in her usual spot. Everything was normal. It was sunny outside, and I sat down near the enormous window to watch the bay. The next moment, the sky was black and starry, my tea was gone, and the bar was vacated. Downtown San Francisco shone brilliantly across the waters, and cars flew in gold and red flurries across the bridge.

Despite all of this evidence to the contrary, I thought for a moment that I was going blind, with the sudden rush of darkness and shadows taking place of the sun that I felt like I just sat down in. I stood up and felt my pant legs stick to me –I had wet myself. Stumbling downstairs I saw that Leeroy was gone as well, not having bothered to look up the stairs before closing.

The jukebox glowed solitary in the darkness next to the bar like some neon monolith, reflected by the window. All other lights were off, chairs and tables illuminated in ghostly orange and green. I don't know if he had forgotten to turn it off, or if it was always on.

Thankfully the front door opened outward from the inside, and locked after I shut it behind me. My watch read 2:00 AM. I quickly drove home, and I somehow came to the conclusion that I had fallen asleep, even though I had clearly drank my iced tea. Disturbed, I decided that the reason for this episode was because I was still very tired, and when I got back to the apartment I, like a complete idiot, took another one of those pills, and was asleep until noon the next day. Only after this second pill did I make the connection, and by this time it was too late. I would lose consciousness and regain it doing menial tasks around the apartment, or be walking down the sidewalk outside in the rain, or be drunk at the bar. I resolved to barricade myself within my apartment until this wore off, but the pills must've been very strong, for this lasted longer than I thought, and they had not yet reached the peak of their effectiveness.

<u>Chapter 11</u>

"Where did you get these from, Don?" I demanded over the phone. I had already lapsed three times that day. The couch, several chairs and the dining table blocked both the front door and the balcony entrance.

"I don't know, from the hospital. They worked fine on me. What's the problem?"

"Any strange side effects?"

"None that I experienced. Are you sure that you're – "

"Yes. Yes. I'll be fine. I just need... a few days."

"Sure, kid. Get some rest."

I tried. It was exhausting to be at one place and then another in the blink of an eye with the sudden passage of several hours. I would sometimes feel completely spent and sweaty, as if I'd run a mile, after only having been sitting down in the same spot for what had felt like a minute before. Despite my blocking myself in, I at one point opened my fridge to find it stocked full of amenities and exotic food that I never usually buy. I usually ate scantily: deli meat sandwiches and pasta were my daily fare, but now my fridge overflowed with durians, pomegranates, soft and hard cheeses and all manner of expensive and unusual food. This meant that I was roaming around without my own knowledge. It was like I was fighting over my own body, and someone else had possessed me in these lapses of cognizance and was furious that I was trying so hard to keep them contained. I found my bathroom overflowing, the sink and bathtub both filled to the brim and spilling out. I found my sheets torn up and slashed. A huge crack appeared in my balcony sliding door. I was at a total loss for how to combat this ailment without admitting myself to a psych ward.

Eventually, however, blackouts began to appear less and less. As my first day of full awareness came to a close, I felt a huge sense of relief, thinking the battle was over – but there were two last slips to be had, and the most outrageous ones at that.

At around four in the morning I awoke to a harsh breeze and saltwater droplets tapping my face, shrouded in total darkness. I was frigid, wearing sweats and a hoodie, and standing barefoot in long grass. It took me a minute to realize, but I was on some cliffs, overlooking what seemed like a complete abyss, with the truck parked a ways behind me.

Roaring, black oblivion. Endless nothingness, cacophonous shadow of night that hid the rise and fall of liquid mountains in the dark, while underneath the waves slept still the final secrets of the world. A true evil biting away at the corners of what dry sanctuary yet escaped its wrath with rhythmic kisses to repeat to the end of time. The ocean.

I stood completely still as my eyes adjusted and I recognized the sound of tumbling waves exploding in the darkness and made out below me the dark shadows of pools of foam coagulating and dissipating. The horizon was endless, the water solemn and unrevealing save for the slivers of gray and black reflection of what moon there was sliding and turning in the surf. I was totally alone. The lights of the city were barely discernible over the hills a ways to my left, a pale, distant glow solemn in the scene.

I stared into this nightmare until I felt the wind draw jagged deltas of tears from the corners of my eyes back across my cheekbones. I slowly turned and walked back to the car, trembling, and found a road away from that place. I had to stop for gas on the way back into the city and the teller at the counter looked me up and down with clear judgment on her face as I slowly found the money to pay.

I got to downtown San Francisco just as the sun was beginning to peek over the horizon. And as I drove down the main streets, going slowly and safely as I possibly could, desperately hoping to arrive home before I should lapse again, I was in the next moment splayed out on the front steps of some small cathedral on the opposite end of town. The truck was thankfully parked, haphazardly as it was, nearby behind me on the curb.

The church was surrounded by small and broken buildings and apartments, in an area of the city where broken windows were common. People dressed in stained clothes and dirty garments walked around without even looking down at me as I struggled up. The cracked pavement where I had been laying was sprinkled with red, and I touched my forehead and saw that I was bleeding. I must have tripped. Trash littered the sidewalk, and pigeons flew overhead and perched on the dark spirals of the church. I checked my watch. It was 9:00 in the morning. I must have driven aimlessly for a long time.

In a daze I stood up and felt blood quickly trickle down my face. The cut didn't hurt much, and it looked worse than it was, but I was bleeding more than I had thought I would be. I wandered up the steps and pushed back the large oak doors to find a sign at the entrance room, saying that confessionals were being held today from now until noon, but there was no one else around. I stumbled into a wide, open area of worship, where sunlight was streaming in blue and green rays through stained glass onto empty pews - with a bit of red speckled in, as by now, blood had seeped into my left eye and I had to keep blinking. Christ on his cross watched the doorway from above the pulpit at the far back side of the church from his place upon the organ pipes. It was totally silent until from behind one of the columns a short, wiry man with round glasses, a fat nose, and a thin beard came up from under one of the pews near a depiction of what I believe was the tower of Babel, where it looked like he'd been sweeping, and stretched his back in a pained arch and groaned aloud. He was entirely bald.

He noticed me at the front door, and what was a warm and welcoming smile turned very quickly into a surprised and serious look of concern when he made out my wound. In an instant he crossed the distance between us and pulled me to one of the empty benches, commanding that I stay there while he bustled off somewhere to fetch a dusty, ancient first-aid kit.

"How'd this happen to you?" He asked me as he dabbed the blood from my face with a wet rag, my head bowed slightly for him to wipe away. A bundle of unwrapped gauze sat next to him.

"Fell over," I mumbled. I was so tired - not just from the actual lack of sleep I was getting but these blackouts had been draining in more ways than one. Outside, the sound of tires lazily pulling cars along the asphalt of the street the church was situated on drifted through the doors.

He stopped what he was doing and looked me dead in the eyes. "Are you on something?"

A bit more judgment than I figured priests were supposed to give, especially to strangers, but the thought was in my head one second and out the next. "Was given some...weird medicine. Been making me, uh, briefly lose consciousness. For a few days now." His features softened back to their patriarchal resting state, and he went back to tending my wound.

"How did you end up here?"

"I'm not sure. Just drove around and...woke up outside."

"You haven't been to the church before...are you from around here?"

"No, I live in Berkeley. Near it, sort of. Moved here a while ago." I closed my eyes. "I was in prison," I heard myself say. "I went to prison and had to move after I got out."

Not even a pause or a whiff of judgment in his response. "What were you in prison for?"

"Inciting a riot, if you can believe it. But I had nothing to do with it."

"Ah," he said, as if he remembered something. I couldn't see his face too well since I was still sort of bent toward him, but I could swear he had let out this big smile. He stopped wiping my forehead and carefully took the bloody rag and placed it behind him, picking up the gauze. He unspooled a roll and began to re-roll it into a tight ball. When it was in a sort of square, he took a pair of scissors, cut the loose strands away, and held it to my forehead with one hand while another used medical tape to keep it there.

"All done. You should keep that on until tonight. Change it if you need to." I sat up straight and touched the patch. It was a very kind thing to do, but I probably looked ridiculous. When I looked into a mirror later, I confirmed this. Like an origami white flower glued to my forehead.

"Thank you, really, very much for all this," I reached out and shook his hand, and stood up to leave. I was still a little dizzy but a good deal better for having come inside. "I think I should get going now."

The priest watched me walk away, and I could feel his eyes on my back. I was two steps from the door when he spoke up.

"You know, funny thing," he suddenly slapped his knees and stood up, the bell at the end of his roped belt jingling softly against his garment. I stopped and turned to face him as he walked slowly up to me. "This church," he gestured vaguely behind him to the pews and windows and organ, "it serves a dedicated but pretty small community. Occasionally someone comes in that isn't a regular member of the congregation, but until today, it was never someone I'd recognized before." He was still giving this warm little smile.

"Come along with me," he said, nodding his head to the back of the church, towards the cross. "There's someone I think you'd like to meet."

I immediately fell under the impression that he was now going to try and convert me, which was completely unwelcome and which started to erode my appreciation for his kindness not seconds earlier. "Hey, father, you know, I appreciate it, but I'm not...this really isn't all for me, you know?"

He laughed and shook his head. "No, you don't understand. I think you know my son," and his little smile turned sad. "He, at least, is very familiar with you. I believe you and a few others took to calling him the humorous nickname 'Mr. 3:16' prior to these riots of yours."

Arthur was in the back of the church tending to a small garden when I crash-landed into his world. It was a motley affair put together in the shade of the ancient steeples, and produced sunflowers, corn, tomatoes, daisies, roses, cucumbers, mushrooms, strawberries, blackberries and beans. Everything blended into another, and when you opened the back door into this little private haven, hidden away in a hall situated behind the church organ, the path turned immediately into tilled dirt with your first step outside. It smelled wonderful.

Father Brian led me through the maze of unorganized foliage and crop to Arthur on his knees digging out the space for some new flowers, wearing a baseball hat and overalls. Brian wore a small rosary around his waist with bells attached to it, which dinged softly against his knee with each step. At the sound of us approaching, Arthur stopped and turned, shading his eyes with one gloved hand. When he saw me behind his father his eyebrows furrowed in recognition, then disbelief, his mouth twisted and turned into a hideous, very loud swear, and his eyes flared up with unexpected, white-hot rage. He jumped up and turned the trowel in his hand as if to bring it down upon my head. Thankfully Brian was there to stop him.

"How did he get here? Why is he here?" Arthur fumed. I took a few steps back as the small but impressive priest backed his child down.

"He did not know who lived here until he revealed himself to me. Put that away." A stern but effective command, and Arthur was immediately cowed. He turned only slightly more docile and the trowel fell into the dirt. He wouldn't even look at me.

"I won't speak to him. Why is he here? What does he want?"

"The riots that have plagued you chase him as well." He put a hand on Arthur's arm. "You must give it a chance.

What are the odds that he would stumble upon this place and find you?"

Arthur was quiet. Father Brian turned to me over his shoulder and asked me politely to wait inside the church for a moment. I could have run away then, and the whole thing would have been over with, but I was completely floored that Mr. 3:16 was in San Francisco. That another person, a fairly major figure at that, who had experienced those riots was here...and that I'd somehow managed to run into him the way that I did. I sat in the pews for around ten minutes until Brian came to retrieve me. By this time the sunlight had begun to come in through the stained glass at a different angle, and now showered the interior in gold and pink.

"My son is getting dressed and will meet us in my office." He appeared out of the darkness into a cherry spotlight. "He is nervous, but that is to be expected, no?" He shrugged casually, as if of course this sequence of events was normal. "I imagine you are as well."

"I'm starting to think I'm still unconscious on the sidewalk outside somewhere." He laughed, and the echoes laughed back and forth at one another for a few seconds, then ascended up to the bell tower into oblivion.

"He is shocked as well. You must forgive him for his initial reaction. He has...bad memories of those times. But, of course, so do you." I recalled the rumors that 3:16 had fallen victim to some of the worse fighting that took place during the later hours of the riots, but like everyone else, what happened to him afterward had been a total mystery.

"He seems to think that I'm the one responsible for what he went through." Brian nodded sadly. "And perhaps you can now correct that."

As I followed the gnomish priest back into the housing where he and Arthur presumably lived, I thought back on my relationship with Mr. 3:16. Truth be told, there wasn't one - we had not been colleagues or even formally acquainted as far as I could remember. I'd never even spoken to him, but I know of him. Everyone did. Every college campus seems to have some religious adherent of some description who'll shout oaths and gospel somewhere, but rarely was that person a fellow student at said school and rarely were they dressed in formal garb in doing so. Arthur was, in that way, sort of a local figure. He was more removed from the movement that caused all of the violence than anyone else, and vehemently attacked it at every opportunity. He spoke ill of me, but I couldn't care less about him. What he perceived of me I had not the slightest idea, but maybe by hearing what he thought of me I would be in a better place to understand why I was still dealing with people like Thomas, people who were still so obsessed with the whole thing.

Father Brian's office was a humble little room in the back of their cottage, with windows on either side open and a floor fan turning lazily to and fro. The curtains were flapping on either end of the room, and would rise up in waves each time the fan turned its head towards them. The walls were seafoam green and bumpy. His desk was sizable and old, a single solid piece of wood completely covered in the rings you'd get when you leave a glass on the table without a coaster. Several dirty mugs stained brown with coffee were at the corner of his desk, and what papers there were had been anchored by a glass paperweight, yet the wind flowing around them made it seem like they were suddenly brought to life and trying to escape with vigor every ten to twelve seconds. Arthur was sitting at one of the two plastic chairs in front of the desk. He had dressed into his priestly garb, a black suit with the white collar bit showing. I sat down next to him, and he did not turn to look at me.

Brian sat down with a grunt, and beamed at the two of us. He looked reproachful at Arthur when his hard glare did not dissipate. "Arthur, you must realize the good providence of such a meeting. Such obstinacy will make any chance of reconciliation all the more difficult."

"I understand that," His son replied through gritted teeth, "but it does not make it any easier. Why do we need to even talk? Why can't he just leave and let it be?" I was in full agreement here: this whole thing was sort of ridiculous, and I opened my mouth to say so, but Brian would have none of it.

"That would be foolish. This is meant to be."

"What do you even want me to say?"

"Why not start with a question? What would you have wanted to ask him?"

Arthur looked down at his lap and was silent. It remained this way until Brian slapped his knees and stood up.

"Perhaps it will be better if I am not here. I will wait outside of the room." My eyes darted frantically around the office to see what weapons Arthur may lurch for as soon as the door shut behind Father Brian, but thankfully the only heavy item within reach was the paperweight, and even then it was closer to me than to him. I tried to signal frantically with my eyes to Brian as he left, but he waved his hand and smiled that calm, inappropriate smile.

"Right outside the door," he said, and closed it behind him.

The uncomfortable air in the room grew even thicker without his father there to facilitate conversation. Neither of us were even in the slightest bit willing to talk. We were quiet for about five full, long minutes, until I finally, out of boredom, said aloud – eyes fully on the paperweight – "Why do you blame me?"

"Who else is there?" He responded immediately. He turned his head and looked at me. Looking directly at him, I was surprised at how old he looked. His face was long and handsome, and the steel-blue shade of incoming facial hair peppered his chin and upper lip. But under his eyes were purple bags and his thin blonde hair dropped down his forehead. His eyes were brown, and his left one had a small streak of hazel on the outer rim that bridged the pupil to the iris.

"I didn't hurt you, physically, in any way. I didn't hurt anyone."

"I'm not mad about that," he scoffed. "That was just a couple of idiot kids. What makes me so mad is that you sat by and watched everything unfold, and didn't care what happened. You could've stopped all of that if you just *said* something."

That took me aback. He placed full responsibility on me because I didn't act to stop anything? "That makes no sense. I didn't put it into motion. Things happened without me knowing, what could I have possibly done?"

"You were the one at the top, right next to that *whore* Elizabeth and that *freak* Dead Richard. You really think that people would've still been killed or hurt if you had said that it was all pointless?"

I was still desperately trying to understand him. To get a look into another view of that night - the idea that I might finally have some insight into what had happened from someone on the outside brought about a sudden, unexpected excitement in me. "You really think I could've done anything?"

"I remember," he leaned back in his chair, eyes still locked on me, "that speech they gave you to read out loud. All that inciting crap. What did you say again?"

"I don't remember."

"I do. Something about how unfair it all was. How this was just the beginning, and how it would spread to other cities. Tell me that doesn't make you cringe just thinking about it."

"I couldn't have turned them down."

"Yes you could, you fucking coward," he hissed. "You just let people get hurt and die."

No wonder he didn't have any friends in college. All of that preaching in front of the library made him very unpopular. Where was his martyrdom? In truth he had that beating coming for a long time.

"The circumstances were such that I was swept along by this whole thing. By the time they gave me those speeches I didn't realize my position was, I don't know, lofty and high-up until it was all over."

He looked hard at me. Trying to see whether or not I was telling the truth. "You didn't know your role in all of this?"

"Not until they put me in jail."

"How did you even get involved, then?"

"Elizabeth."

He sneered. "What, were you fucking her?"

"No. She started bothering me. Bringing me places that I didn't want to go."

"But you *did* go along. And you could've just ignored her."

"The people..." I faltered. "I don't know, they seemed interesting. What they were doing was out of the ordinary. But I always thought that my place was more like..."

"...Whose?"

"Richard's. He never did or said anything. But he was always there. Can you tell me why? How did they interpret me? Why did they want me to be so important?"

Me asking this, and the urgency that must have come through my voice, seemed to throw him for a loop, and persuaded him that I really did not have any idea what was going on during that time. "You didn't – I mean you don't know?"

"I've only heard bits and pieces. Never why."

"It was always vague. You just seemed so...unaffected. They really played off of that."

"*Unaffected?*"

"Nothing bothered you. No goals or anything. You just lived day to day in like a pattern. At least, that's what they said. You 'refused to live', that was it. That was their big tagline. You were 'rebelling against the system you were placed in'. Some nonsensical crap like that."

I just sat there. He regarded me suspiciously.

"I remember reading something about how you had a set schedule," he shifted in his chair after I didn't say anything. "You'd get up at a certain time, brush your teeth at a certain time, eat only certain foods, and so on. You didn't even have any real friends."

"It doesn't make any sense," I said, completely dumbfounded. "At all."

"What doesn't?"

"Them. It...I don't care." I waved it off. "It really doesn't matter, I guess. It's over and done with."

"You can say that," he leaned back, "but there are people out there who still keep up with what happened."

"Yeah, I know. I've met them. They're fanatics and they should only be ignored until they move onto something else." I turned to him. His hard face had softened a little bit. "Have you had any trouble with people like that?"

He considered me before answering. "Only a little. Earlier on, when the news was still fresh. They'd come to service and try to rile people up or ask me questions, but they never got very far. It's probably been harder for you."

We were both silent for a bit. I began to recognize the scent of Arthur's garden wafting through the windows. Rain was coming, too. You could smell it with the wet soil.

"For what it's worth, I am sorry that that happened to you," I ventured. Perhaps if I came off as sympathetic or apologetic he'd be less inclined to violence against me. Really

I didn't blame myself at all for what he went through, and to an extent, perhaps he deserved it.

"Yeah, well." He rubbed the back of his neck, and contemplated the dirty mugs on his father's desk. "Me too."

We listened to the sound of rain starting to lightly fall on the roof above us, then with greater force as the storm loomed overhead. Behind, the sound of footsteps shuffling away from the door indicated that Brian's attention was needed elsewhere.

"God," Arthur suddenly snapped, "He should really clean up in here."

Chapter 12

The next time I saw Don I gave him back the pills and told him everything I had experienced, up to me meeting Arthur. He was completely appalled.

"Are you serious?" We were in a company truck on the way to a gas station downtown.

"Where did you get these?" He gave me some hospital name I'd never heard of.

"I've never gone through anything like that before in my life. My family has no history of anything like that either."

He didn't say anything. I think he was at a complete loss for words. That night at work he received a very angry call from Adelaide because he had missed one of his daughter's school ballet recitals. He apologized, but tersely said that he was working, and hung up. He was fine during the actual job, but after it was finished he asked me if I felt like getting a drink. I understood that he didn't want to go home yet, so we went to the bar. Outside of the front door a picture of the curly-haired porn scholar was posted, with a caption saying "do not let onto the premises". We walked inside and for the first time in what must have been four or so months the woman dressed in robes was there, sitting at the table where the porn scholar used to sit, triumphantly drinking a martini and reading a large leather-bound book.

I knew that this change had only occurred because Leeroy was the new bartender, and because he was spineless. There was nothing I could do about it, and I didn't want to put myself in a compromising position, but this cemented what I had feared. With Lorelei's vanishment this place had begun to slowly lose its delicate poise. A trend of patrons being banished from, or abandoning the bar. She was the catalyst – following her was Eddie, and now the scholar. I was deeply troubled, but what could I do to stop it?

The three in the back of the room had not noticed the change, and were talking as usual. Walker had his head down in his arms and was making a low moaning sound. Louis, staring at him, asked George a question.

"How much you say he drank, George?"

George, mid-sip, put down his beer. "Well, you remember Sam?

Louis glanced over at him. "Marine Corps Sam?"

"The very same."

"What about him?"

"Well. Sam was in town last night. And him and Walker here went out to the bars."

I saw Louis' eyes widen. "Did you go with them?"

"Nope. I was at the gym."

"You and the fucking gym. How much did he have to drink?"

"Sammy boy told me that Walker here tried to keep pace with him, and, well," George slapped Walker on the back here, hard, eliciting nothing less than a scream and the sound of a repressed vomit from beneath his arms. "Sam called it a night when he lost count of how many times he'd pulled Walker out from wandering into the street, and shoved him into a taxi."

Louis shook his head. "The infinite hubris of man." George nodded in agreement.

Walker gave a small cry. "I'm fighting for my life."

"Well why did you come out to the bar today, you dope?"

I could barely hear Walker now. "Hair of the dog."

"That only works when you can keep it down, dummy. You need to get some water in you."

Upstairs Benjamin and Katie were talking quietly to one another in tones far more rushed than usual. Don and I took a spot by the window. It was sprinkling a little bit outside in the dark. We both drank quietly as the drops began to hit and spray across the glass with more strength.

Don finished his drink and sat looking out for a bit, elbow on table, propping up his head. His eyes were tired, but not the kind of fatigue you get from physical work. He'd been bothered by something. It had been on his mind for a while.

I tried to reassure myself that I was overthinking this by asking him out loud "Are you alright?"

He glanced back over at me and I could tell that he forgot I was there. He rubbed his face with both of his hands. "Yeah kid," I heard him mumble. "Yeah, I'm alright."

We left soon after. He departed with a quick smile and drove off into the night to confront his angry wife and his unmentioned, unknowable anxieties. I hoped that he would turn out okay.

As for Arthur, our relationship did not evolve very quickly into an amicable one, and in its later stages we had reached a silent, mutual understanding that there were aspects of one another that we simply did not like. I thought him bombastic and morally arrogant, and he in turn saw me as apathetic and ethically bankrupt. But regardless of the early animosity, Father Brian was right in that we were bound by our experiences – experiences that Arthur had thought I shared some guilt in crafting. With the first awkward meeting that notion was challenged. But I came away from it not having any better understanding of my role in the riots aside from the cryptic explanation that he had provided me.

I started to come to services there about a week or so after the side-effects of those pills had finally stopped. I don't know if I expected much out of this, but in any case we began to converse more.

Even if you didn't know Arthur, and hadn't experienced his natural-born animosity firsthand, you could tell by looking at him that there was something bubbling up under the surface. His entire body was tense, and when he thought he wasn't being watched, his eyes became much sharper - beady little holes that flared with some unknowable resentment or contempt that would drift over a morning service in his church, either looking for something among the parish or aware of something that no one else seemed cognisant of. Frankly, if you watched him long enough you could find yourself wondering if he had ever experienced a moment of happiness in his life. He was visibly wound up, as if always ready for someone to throw a punch, or if he had grown impatient with someone he was speaking with, and you had to question why no one had just sat him down at some point and simply asked what his problem was. What the ultimate source of his frustration was I could only guess at. But for the first few times I went and visited, he would shut himself away immediately after the service had ended and refuse to speak to me. Brian would shake his crystal ball of a head sadly and ask me to try again the next week. I suppose Arthur, and our strange connection to one another, was interesting enough to warrant my interest to a point.

On around my fifth visit to the cathedral, and having not had any more conversations with him, I was among the last to leave when he called out and asked me to accompany him to the church garden. It must have been the summer, because while you could never really tell what season or even what month it was in San Francisco without paying close attention, it was outrageously hot that day. The sunflowers were wilting and the tomatoes seemed fit to burst with the heat at any second, and after removing his frock Arthur was furiously watering them down with a hose.

I stood there for a few moments until he threw a watering can at me. "Be useful."

The sheer size of the garden took us around twenty minutes to get everything sufficiently watered down, and by the end of it we were drenched with sweat. We retreated into the shade aside the church and sat there cooling off.

Despite the heat of the day the wind carried with it the salt of the ocean and it was pleasant. Hummingbirds were gathered around some still dripping flowers at the far end of the bed.

"Look," Arthur wiped his forehead with the back of his forearm, "How much longer are you going to keep coming here?"

"I don't know. Brian seemed to think that it was a good idea."

"Well, do you?"

I shrugged.

"That's your problem," he sniffed. "You have zero conviction. No idea what you're doing."

I didn't answer. A strong breeze had just come through the reeds and I sat there enjoying it - with how hot it had been you could swear steam was rising off of us. He looked at me for a second more and then got up and dusted himself off and walked off to the backside of the church, around where Brian's office was situated. I got up and followed.

You wouldn't have been able to tell because of the way the streets and courtyard wall were laid out, but far behind the church and still enclosed in the courtyard there was a small grove of trees, five of them total. They were tall and provided enough foliage to shade the ground below, and tying them together in the upper canopy was a network of horribly thorny vines, possibly the result of some fungal infection. In the space between them on the ground, about twenty feet by twenty feet, was a pile of bricks and dirt. Arthur didn't notice that I followed him, and picking up a pair of gloves on the ground and grabbing a shovel he got to work digging. He jumped into the ground and disappeared, until I saw the shovel tip hop up out of the grass and toss out dirt. He had been working on a deep ditch.

Once again I stood there awkwardly for a minute or two until he paused to wipe the sweat off of his forehead and spotted me.

"*What?*" He demanded. I guess he had expected me to turn around and go home.

"What are you building here?"

He got back to shoveling and mumbled out an answer to me. "It's gonna be...like a ceremony thing."

"Oh?"

"It'd be nice to hold some small sermons or weddings out here in the spring."

"Plenty of free space. How long have you been working on this for?"

"Few months." I walked over and jumped over the ditch and picked up a saw that had been in the dirt.

"If you're going to hang around, use that to trim the roots." He commanded from below. He tossed his head backward to indicate where they were. "They're pretty thick and they're in the way."

"Alright." I had nothing else to do that day. Besides, I was no stranger to physical work and my intuition told me that Arthur was the sort who approved of someone who could tax themselves with no whining. I was correct. Two hours later the troublesome roots had been carved away and he seemed pleased for the first time since I had met him. He quickly remembered himself, though, and only muttered out a grunt of "Alright job I guess", and went back to digging. I didn't want to overstay my welcome, so I ended the day here.

> *We're shuffling on in solemn silence.*
> *Damp and gloom. Night without end.*
> *But suddenly – so melodiously –*
> *An automobile comes round the bend.*

> *Its paint of shimmering glossy black,*
> *Its crystal facets shining bright;*
> *Into the dark it stretches out,*
> *Two broad angelic wings of white.*

A younger man had accompanied the lady dressed in robes to the bar today, and the unusual sound of both her laughter and his new voice was immediately jarring to the regulars. Her friend was dressed in a similarly outlandish fashion, with large hoop earrings, dyed blue hair, and a brown jacket a professor might wear, with elbow padding. He must've been half the other one's age. When they came in, she had bustled over to the jukebox to show it off to her guest, who laughed shrilly with delight when she put on a poem. He had tried to talk to Leeroy about some nonsense, his *inspiration* for such a *unique* idea, which was completely and totally ignored until the young man sheepishly asked for a drink. What they were talking about I couldn't say, but what I do remember is how I looked around the rest of the bar and noticed that the others were watching them. Louis, Walker, George, and Leeroy. They made no effort to hide it. I was confused, because the woman and her friend weren't being particularly loud or disruptive. I realized that they were sizing the newcomer up. Was he worthy to take the place of the scholar who had been removed at the behest of the older woman? Did he have a right to sit at the bar?

Of course, I might've been overthinking it. He did stand out a lot, after all, and eventually the boys returned to their own musings and Leeroy returned to reading his magazine. Still, for a moment it seemed like I was not alone in understanding the unspoken significance of this place – that the bar was special, and that only those deemed deserving might be given a seat here. I began to wonder if I had been watched in the early days when I first started coming here, before I became a regular. Later on that day, when Katie and Ben descended from their place upstairs, Katie turned a sharp eye to the newcomer and whispered something to her boyfriend. He looked over, smiled, and whispered something back.

Chapter 13

I would have liked for things to have returned back to a rhythmic normalcy after all of this, but around this time I received a very ugly and unwelcome phone call from my old university registrar. How they found my number I have no idea, but I was told in very lawyerly terms that I had been ordered by a local court to present to the university president, in person, a letter of apology for my part in the riots. I hung up on them. They called back with the same speech. I hung up again. The fifth time they called their voice had become a lot brisker. I was deeply offended because this was by no means necessary or required. They just wanted some good PR. The riots must've hit them harder than I thought, and this all came just as I was starting to feel like that bunk could finally start being forgotten.

"Now look –" they began. I cut them off.

"No. Do not call me again."

"You've been court ordered – "

"I do not care. I will not be coming."

"We reserve the right to – " I hung up once more.

Ten minutes later, they called again. A different voice was on the phone, a woman's.

"Hello?"

"Wait a minute. We can make you an offer."

"You have nothing to offer. I am not coming back. And I am certainly not apologizing."

"We've been authorized to remove your school record if you comply. It'll be as if you never studied here."

This gave me pause. Disassociating myself with the school would be a great way to further bury my connection to the protests, and if they were on board it'd be a big help. I took a second to think. "But a quick search online will bring up my name and dozens of articles."

"Well, we can't do anything about that. But what we can do is confirm that the matter has been settled, instead of saying that you're ignoring court summons and bringing you further attention."

I felt the blood drain from my face in indignation. "Are you blackmailing me?"

"Not at all. Just stating the facts."

I was livid. The person on the other end must've been able to tell.

"We will pay for your travel out here. It will take no longer than one hour."

It appeared that I was cornered. If I ignored them I would be in trouble with the law again. If I accepted it and went along not only would it decimate my pride but I would be back on campus, presumably around people who might recognize me.

Suddenly, for some reason, I felt the need to ask for Arthur's advice. He was in the riots, he went to that school. Perhaps he could shed some wisdom on the matter. Perhaps he would feel the same righteous furor that I did.

"I...I will call you back."

"You have twenty four –"

"*I'll contact you* when I have an answer. No earlier. Expect to make some compromises." And for the last time I hung up.

The next day was Sunday, so I drove over to mass with some vague idea in mind of how to bring up my situation to Arthur. However, as I arrived right after morning Mass concluded, I would need to wait patiently until Grandma Alejandra had had her say with him - a peculiar, almost ritualistic event that seemed designed to make Arthur something of a spectacle and which should have in theory humbled him.

Once a week, Arthur was verbally assailed by an ancient Mexican abuela who was a long time attendee of the church.

She would mutter to him in Spanish and broken English after Mass every Sunday, always wearing a large sun hat and a floral mumu, shaking her wrinkled fists at him in a quiet rage. Arthur would often simply just stand there and take it until she tired herself out.

"What's that all about?" I'd asked once, as she shuffled out of the main room. Arthur, unbothered, was putting away the bibles that had been left on pews.

"Around half a year ago I gave her granddaughter some advice that she did not agree with."

"She really seems to have it in for you."

"Should've seen her in the beginning. Brian had to stop her from beating me with her cane."

"Why does she keep coming here?"

"She used to say it was because she liked Father Brian's sermons so much. But recently she's told me that she will plague me until the day I die." Despite this, he seemed completely unbothered, and that tension that was otherwise always in him vanished whenever Alejandra gave him a piece of her mind.

That was a little while ago. Today the old woman shook her cane more animatedly than usual and spat while speaking, but she eventually tired herself out and was helped to the door by Brian, who murmured words of encouragement and asked for her forgiveness for whatever transgression Arthur had committed. She waved him off.

"I need your advice on something." Arthur looked up, surprised, from behind the podium where he'd be sweeping.

I followed him back to the church kitchen and laid out the situation. When I explained my predicament to him, Arthur's face clouded. I had half expected him to laugh and tell me that I'd deserved what was coming to me, but his ears got flushed and soon he was shouting indignantly to no one but himself.

"Who the hell do they think they *are*?" He was working himself up while brewing tea. The church kitchen was clean, almost spotless, in stark contrast to Brian's quarters. Arthur must've handled the upkeep here, too. "What're you going to do?"

If there was one thing that Arthur liked, I was beginning to understand, it was feeling like the underdog. He could forgo all negative opinions of me if he felt that some greater injustice was being done and that there was a chance to fight back against whatever the transgressor may have been.

"I don't know. They're offering to remove my record from the school."

"You never graduated, did you?" He poured me green tea and went back to the sink.

"No. I think I had like two semesters left when I went to jail. Never considered going back. Did you?"

"No."

"I'm tempted to take them up on it, just so they'll leave me alone and not raise any sort of stink. But it's not like they can erase everything. People would still be able to look me up if they wanted."

Arthur thought for a moment. "This really is just all for them. You get nothing out of it."

"Yeah."

"Trying to frame erasing your record as like, a favor to you, is stupid. It's insulting." He tapped his own glass in frustration. After a moment he shook his head, not even having sipped it, and poured it out in the sink, restless. "Is the court order thing real?"

"Probably not. I think what they're really trying to do is force me to come in, or they'll keep talking about me in negative terms. If I show up, then they'll at least refuse to comment on me..or if they do, they won't have much more to say. The matter will be settled on their terms."

"Is that a deal you're willing to take?"

"I don't know. I don't really know how much they've already said about me. And I don't really want to go back."

"Can't blame you."

Brian was humming to himself in the other room. I had begun to notice that Brian always got into a good mood whenever Arthur and I talked because I don't think Arthur had many friends. It also provided enough warning to

Arthur not to swear loudly, which I was sure he would have gratuitously if Brian was not nearby.

"What's the best deal you can get from them, you think?" He asked after a moment of pondering. He was washing his glass out.

"They offered to pay for my flight tickets. That's about it."

He snorted. "Not nearly enough. If they're desperate enough to ask you to send them an apology, they'll shell out more. I think this whole court order thing is made up so they don't have to."

"What do you think I should ask for? If I decide to go through with it," I added.

Arthur placed his cup on the drying rack and walked slowly around the table, absentmindedly cracking each of his knuckles in thought.

"Here's what I'd do," He suddenly pulled out a chair and sat down across from me, hunched over like he was hatching some conspiracy. "Ask for a full refund of your tuition. Tell them no cameras. No press. A ride from and to the airport. *And* they can't publicize the meeting, unless to put you in a good light."

That was a lot to ask. "Man, I dunno. Who knows if they'll keep their word even if they do agree?"

"If they end up pulling something dirty you can always go and tell everyone that they lied about a court order just to get you out there. It'd look way worse for them. Plus you'd have no reason to lie about it because you don't want to go back there in the first place."

"You really think so?"

"Just imagine how much they'd get stung if it got out that they lied about something like that." He muttered a swear under his breath. He seemed angrier about this than I was.

I didn't want to go back, but Arthur was right. The school seemed desperate. It wouldn't last very long - and I could potentially get them to stop speaking poorly of me, as I could only assume they had been. The refunded tuition would be an added bonus.

I thought it over and shook my head. "I hate to go back out there, but I'll call them and see what we can arrange." I was lucky enough that Don had requested off of work for the next week, and because I was his partner, I didn't have to clock in unless I asked to tag along with another crew.

"You ever meet President DuCard?" Arthur asked suddenly.

I racked my brain. Brief images of a tall, balding man in three piece suits flashed in my memory, but nothing concrete. He wore trademark red-framed glasses in every publicity photo I ever saw him in. "Well, uh, no. Not personally. I saw him at a few student events, but that's it."

"I met him two or three times. Everyone always liked him. Maybe he'll be nice."

"Maybe."

I called the registrar back that night and laid out my demands. The person on the other line was extremely hesitant, but after talking it over with their superiors, they agreed to everything. Arthur had been right. I hadn't asked for the ride from and to the airport, though. I didn't want one of their chauffeurs.

They still needed to express some semblance of control, though, so I was given orders on how to proceed after they agreed to everything. "You'll arrive here tomorrow at noon. Your meeting will take place at 1:00. It will last no longer than five minutes."

"I come in, sign a paper, and leave. I will be reading it before signing it, however."

"You'd be stupid not to," the person on the other end laughed at me.

"And no press whatsoever. Any and all articles published must be done after I return to Berkeley and must not make disparaging remarks about me."

"Fine."

Then I thought of something. "The student body must not be made aware of my visit until after I am already gone, and through no official announcement. Media channels only."

The other side of the line got very quiet. After a moment, they tersely replied, "We'll see to it." I had no idea what might've been getting planned right up to that point, but I was very glad that I had mentioned that.

"And in return for this -" I was interrupted.

"The University will make no comments on your relation to the events of which you are submitting a formal apology for. Yes. Are you quite finished?" All of the polite pretense of the earlier calls had totally evaporated by this point and it was like talking to an exhausted customer service representative. A small part of me felt bad for putting them through the ringer on what I wanted, but it was only a very, very small part.

"In addition to the monetary repayments we have agreed upon. I want all of what we have discussed on paper on the president's desk next to this apology notice."

"It will be there. Are we done?"

"One final thing."

"What?"

"If you backslide on any of these agreements, I will submit to student and local newspapers proof of your lying of having obtained a court summons for my apology. I expect the tickets shortly." And I hung up. I had no such proof, but a quick inquiry into the state court would bring that up in no time. Whoever it was that thought this plot up hadn't really been thinking at all.

The next morning I took a cab to the airport, boarded my plane, and during the long flight tried to figure out how this would all go. The ticket to return back to California was slated for later in the afternoon on the same day, but I could wait in the airport for as long as I needed after our meeting concluded. I was wearing a hooded sweatshirt and jeans which I made sure I had purchased after I'd moved to California. I also made sure to check what month it was before flying out - it was October, so the Fall semester would be in session. But if I was quick, no one would recognize me. Besides, most of the students there hadn't seen me before anyways, given how long it'd been since this all occurred.

Appalachia is a rocky scar littered with collapsed sheds hidden away by thick rows of thin trees. You can feel that every hill and field is haunted by the ghosts of past childhoods. Hidden in plain sight, behind dilapidated restaurants and grazing horses, are the deadly phantoms of nostalgia. They will take hold of you if you are not careful, and with every lonely home and small lake you pass you will feel an inexplicable swelling in your throat. As I took the taxi from on the long drive to campus, I resisted that feeling and instead was overcome by a surprising feeling of regret: not that I had come back here, but that I had been forced to leave at all. As I got closer and closer to the building where the president's office was situated, I passed many landmarks that I had lazily trudged by as a student - diners, statues, thrift stores. Each place was as gray and colorless as it had been in my memory.

The air was cold, dry, and smelled like car exhaust and wet dead leaves, and crossing the street from where I'd been dropped I quickly hurried inside, crossed the atrium floor patterned with the school colors and rushed up one of the grand staircases. So far, no one had even looked at me. I hadn't even taken the time to notice all of the welcome-back-to-school banners and decorations that were still hanging up.

I took a moment to look down into the hall from atop the stairwell. I couldn't help but instantly notice how I stood out from all of them, the students. They were gathered in groups, laughing, or running to and from classes. Some looked very young, younger than I remember being when I was a freshman. They all looked so happy and excited. Meanwhile I was scurrying through them like some shady, suspicious, reviled character. I turned away.

The president's office had thankfully been fully informed and ready, so the door to the waiting room was quickly locked after my entrance and the blinds closed. One of the women who greeted me was a little plump with a head of great white frizzy hair. She was very polite despite knowing who I was, but I was not about to be tricked into anything.

"How was your flight? Would you like anything to drink?"

"No thank you. Is President DuCard ready?"

"Let me just go and make sure. Please, make yourself comfortable." I remained standing, and close to the door just in case. She returned with a smile and I followed her in.

Ducard sat behind a large oak desk in a room with a huge glass window to his backside, the walls to our left and right adorned with photos, framed newspaper clippings of sports championships, ribbons, banners, and of course degrees. His hands were folded in front of him and he was watching me, unsmiling. He was wearing the red glasses I'd seen so often in publicity photos, but he had lost much more hair. What was once a shallow patch of skin atop his head was now a pronounced, and dare I say even glistening, bald spot. I probably had some responsibility in that, and for a second I wondered if he was only demanding this apology as part of a personal vendetta for exacerbating his receding hairline. I nodded at him and he tipped his head once in acknowledgement. Unfortunately the angle of light was such that it gleamed off of his scalp.

I picked up the paper and glanced it over. It was as we had all agreed on over the phone, so I signed it, nodded once more, took a copy, and walked out. That was it - painless, quick and surgical. I departed the building and was comfortably outside, away from curious eyes.

The whole process took, from getting out of my taxi to returning to the street, maybe ten minutes, so I had a good amount of time before the flight back home. I crossed the street outside and remembered that about a block away was one of the houses that had burned down. Since no one had yet approached me, and I for all intents and purposes seemed like a stranger here, I decided to walk over and look at what remained.

A small parking lot for the buildings it was wedged between had replaced the ruins which had once smoldered brightly, surrounded by shadows and spectators that screamed and whooped in my memory. The whole scene didn't really look better under gray, wet skies and alone than it did on fire in the black of night crowded by drunken idiots. The decaying brick of both buildings which faced towards the asphalt had on them faded graffiti, rotting blue and green depictions similar to the mural I'd found in San Francisco ages ago. One was a large proclamation in orange and white, screaming "Poor Betty!" in huge, towering letters. Dead flower petals littered the ground underneath it.

I racked my brain. Betty. B&E Betty? She hadn't died. She had suffered some injuries, but nothing life threatening. If she went to jail I didn't hear about it. We had never really even spoken to one another, but I knew that she did manage to make a lot of people angry with her Robin Hood antics...claiming a moral high ground similar to Arthur's but with some tangible, real-world consequences instead of making an ass of yourself in front of the library. Maybe this mural was made more so in response to her assailants never being fully prosecuted, if that was the case.

"Surprised to see you here," someone suddenly called from somewhere above me. The building to the right had a balcony, and someone was leaning over it, grinning broadly, wearing a bucket hat and blue suspenders. My heart jumped and I quickly turned around and walked away.

The day didn't change color or temperature. The plane outbound disappeared into gray clouds it had descended from, and while I was clearly safe now, I was still restless. I hadn't gotten a written commitment for the refund of my tuition, but even that was at the back of my mind. The whole visit passed uneventfully...something was bothering me, but I couldn't place my finger on what. Unable to sleep, I started rummaging through my bag to see if I'd brought anything to read. I pulled out *The Wind in the Willows* and finally finished it before we landed back home.

Chapter 14

I was looking forward to a return to normalcy when I landed, but this wasn't to be the case. In fact, looking back on it, I wonder if I shouldn't have left to fly back east in the first place. As when Lorelei disappeared from the bar, my own absence from Berkeley, even as brief as it was, felt like it disrupted some sort of balance. It was a feeling I did not overcome during the flight and which I tried to shake off as I headed over to the bar.

The only patrons there tonight were the asian girl and Ben and Katie. The latter were, for the first time in memory, sitting on opposite sides of the coffee table separating two couches, and not entwined in each other's arms. I wanted to shake them and demand why they had done this, just what exactly they thought they were doing, but all I could do was sit in the far back corner and watch. They were having what appeared to be the first serious discussion of their entire relationship, and at the end of the night, they walked out, his arm over her shoulders, without as much as a backwards glance. I thought about calling Arthur and asking how the progress had been going with his backyard project, but remembering that I had a shift with Don the next day I thought better of it and headed home.

My empty apartment embraced me and shrouded me from the frustrations of the outside once more as night descended: no calls from the university, no news or annoyances. Before I fell asleep, I took a moment to stand on the porch and watch the city across the bay in the dark. It was alive and vibrant from which great arteries curled across the water on both sides and funneled its citizens to and fro, and I was struck for a second of how similar the glow of the city was to the burst of color from the jukebox in the bar. Both alight with the swirl of souls churning endlessly deep inside - for one, the glow never ceased, but the other, it only came to life when someone was brave enough to ask it to.

Airplanes flew in scarlet comets across the air, the light of stars invisible. It was the first time that I really watched San Francisco from afar. The wind was whipping around my feet and curling the waves below, impenetrable darkness kind enough to reflect the city's beautiful face but never to allow it any farther in. After all that effort, that extra work to get the money to buy an apartment with a porch, only now was I appreciating the view. As if spurred on somehow, a small earthquake shook the area after I went to bed.

The next day Don and I were set to meet at a local library to do some work on the bathrooms, in conjunction with another plumber named Caesare. I had worked with him before. He was an ancient man of Italian descent who, if you believed the rumors, had fled Milan after some involvement with the Red Brigades in the 1970's. His face resembled the back car seat of an elementary school bus - brown, slightly cracked with wear and tear, and blemished with the abuse of time. His eyebrows were so comically large that part of me wondered if they were the result of a rogaine experiment gone awry. They took up half of the space of his forehead, and were meticulously groomed, some days dripping with pomade, the result no doubt of an ancient ritual embedded in his blood decades ago in a young age far away on the other side of the planet and that he never once considered shedding. His eyes never opened all the way, as is the case with very old men, but with a sidewards glance you could just barely make out a startlingly blue color, a sharpness that hinted as to the clarity of his mind. He wasn't a man to be feared, at least not anymore, but he had no trouble reminding you with a simple look, if necessary, that people behind his back affiliated him with terrorists. We did not work together very often, but as with Don, an appearance of quiet, refined masculinity was welcomed and quietly approved of. He called me "killer", for some reason, and occasionally asked when I was going to find myself a girl, apparently forgetting that he had asked me this several times previously.

The library's infrastructure hadn't been touched since the times when Caesare may or may not have been running amok in Italy, and I wasn't looking forward to all of the rust and cracked pipes we would be replacing and throwing away for the greater part of my Thursday. Despite this, I was surprised to find myself anxious to hear some reassuring, pretentious question from Don. All I needed was one offhand remark, one pseudo-philosophical quip for all to be right with the world and the earth to remain stable under my feet.

Caesare appeared, but Don did not. My heart sank as Caesare called the main office to ask where he was. Diligent students passed us on the main floor, hurriedly finding study spaces. Mothers with their children were attending a community event in the kids area off to the side, where someone was doing a show with puppets.

"Didn't clock in this morning. Might be sick or something." Some kid screamed with delight as Caesare closed his phone and walked to the help desk. Reluctantly, I followed him. Not two hours later did I receive a call, just as I had finished removing some faulty lining and brought the replacements over to Caesare. This was going to take a lot longer without a third person on hand, especially considering Caesare's age, so, annoyed, I picked up.

"Where are you?"

"Hey, uh, I'm sorry," Don was out of breath. Not from running, but the kind of exasperation that comes with a pent-up emotional outburst. The kind that drains you and leaves you shaken, and your life balance seemingly on a precipice. You could always tell by the hoarseness of a person's voice, and when I heard it, I felt myself get very tired.

"I need a favor. Please."

"Are you alright?"

"Do you have your truck? Did you drive it to the -"

"Yes. Where are you? Are you okay?"

"I need a ride," he choked and spat something out. Behind him a bird chirped. "I'm at my house."

"I'm still at work with Caesare."

"Let me speak to him." I tapped Caesare, who was muttering at some incorrigible nut, and gave him my phone, desperately hoping that his eyebrow grease wouldn't get smeared on it.

"*Dove sei?*" He snarled into it. They talked for a few minutes more, some in Italian and broken English, and all with his free hand, waving a dirty rag around like it was the flag at the end of a race car track. Finally, he cursed (at least I assumed), and he hung up abruptly, tossing my phone back to me.

"Go." He turned and went back to work.

"You gonna be okay here?" He grunted angrily and waved me off, and after a few more awkward words of thanks, I took my leave and drove to Don's out-of-place baijiu shack. As I pulled in, I spotted him standing on the front porch, two old suitcases in hand. He waved me over. Wordlessly, he tossed the suitcases into the back and climbed into the passenger's seat. For a moment, we didn't move and no one spoke, until, frustrated, he turned to me.

"What? What're you waiting for?"

I finally found my voice. "I've...never seen you in a suit before."

Don was wearing a corduroy suit so dusty that it had made the air in the front seat visibly filthy. It had several sewn-up holes scattered around it, and he was wearing a curled blue tie and black dress pants. All of these articles were in some state of disrepair. He reminded me of a caricature of a down-on-his-luck car salesman. His face was ashen white and his eyes were red with tears of frustration and confusion. He buckled up.

"First time for everything," he laughed awkwardly. I slowly regained my motor functions and drove out onto the street.

Don directed me to drive several miles outside of the city on the opposite end of the bay, at some obscure location that he refused to elaborate on. As we passed through downtown, under old strip-club signs and past bookstores, Don's composure did not improve. He repeatedly straightened his tie, fidgeted with his suit, and tapped his feet, as if he had to keep moving lest his energy become bottled up. He would not look at me. When we finally left the city behind us and began weaving through great, grassy slopes I broke the silence.

"What are you doing, Don?"

He didn't answer immediately. He'd stopped fidgeting and was slumped against the window.

"I'm leaving, kid."

"I can see that. To where? Why?"

"I don't know. I..." He rubbed his eyes and sat up straight, regaining his composure.

"Did you have a fight with your wife?"

"That's not why I'm leaving. I just...I just want to."

"Are you in some kind of danger?"

"No, kid. No danger. I'm fine."

"Then what you're doing makes no sense." I stopped hard on the brakes as a deer leapt out in front of the truck, slamming Don's luggage into my back window and eliciting a strong curse from their owner. I waited to see if anymore followed from the woods, then slowly drove on. Don continued after recomposing himself.

"It makes sense."

"How long are you going to be gone for?"

"I'm not coming back." I looked over at him.

"You have two daughters and a son."

"Don't preach to me. Just drive."

"You're leaving behind your family for no reason whatsoever."

"I have a reason."

"Then what is it? What?"

"I just - I want something more," He deflated. "I want something more. Haven't you ever wanted that?"

In the time that I had known Don, his ramblings about ideology and wisdom never seemed to bleed from idle talk into the stability and composure of his personal life. What I had thought the musings of a bored old man had, it seemed, weighed more heavily on him than I could've known. "At the expense of your family? Have you even thought about this?"

"For weeks and months and years." He was suddenly red faced and flustered. "You know, you know, we talked about this before. This is all I've ever done and I - I can't take it. I can't. Call me a coward or a hypocrite or whatever, but it's my life. Mine, you know? It's the only one I got, and it's been too, just, perfect.. And I've been livin' it like some...like some..." His words faded.

"You're having a midlife crisis." He shook his head and looked away like the accusation offended him. "What about your children?" He was quiet for a minute. We were getting close to the address.

"I just hope maybe they'll understand someday."

Finally we reached it - some dilapidated bus stop. Surrounded by grassy knolls and with a view of the ocean far on the horizon, its roof was partially caved in and the glass bench which had once supported passerbys was long since shattered and the bench legs stood out of the concrete like rusty, orange young tree stumps. I pulled up and Don wordlessly got out of the car and began taking his suitcases from the back. I decided to get out too. He walked over and, putting one of the suitcases down, sat on it and checked his watch. He glanced up at me.

"Don't try to stop me."

"Wasn't gonna."

"I'm not - I don't want you to think I'm a bad guy. Please."

"What else am I supposed to think?"

It was midday. It was very warm out, and as cars appeared on either side of the road you could see the hazy mirage lines rise from them until they got close enough and sped by.

"Where's your bus to?" Don ignored me.

"I'm not going to tell Adelaide."

He looked up at me. "Some town north of here."

"Got a plan?"

"I'll make one."

"Friends?"

"I'll make some."

I was looking hard at him. In that moment, I was furious at him. Had we not had some understanding of one another so long ago? Where did that go? Far better to live a life you can control, wasn't it? And now he was throwing all of that away, as if it had all been for nothing. He was abandoning me to fight this on my own, and I felt betrayed. Why was he doing this?

Hurt, confused and angry, I felt my own hand reach into my pocket and slowly retrieve my truck keys. I heard myself say "Here," and toss them to Don. I couldn't believe it and neither could he. He fumbled in the air and, falling to his knees, managed to catch them.

He looked at the keys in the palm of his hand, cradling them as if they were something precious, and looked back up at me, bewildered.

"Kid, I can't take the truck. What're you doing?"

I stared at them, in-between his enormous, calloused hands. Hands that had done more work than I might in my entire lifetime. Hands that had placed the engagement ring on his wife's finger, had lovingly held three separate babies. Hands that had labored to provide them all food, a home.

Hands that had filled his shack with exotic clutter and oddities from around the world, a growing altar to a life that would never be his to live. And an ugly, fat face that was tired and miserable and guilt-ridden, whose eyes were still puffy with tears and the pores backed up with grease and grime from his filthy trade. For a brief second - without condoning, but perhaps a fraction less condemning - I think I understood him and where he was coming from.

"Just take it."

"I can't -"

"Take the truck, Don." I repeated through gritted teeth. If he asked again I might've changed my mind.

He slowly stood up, and suddenly, rushing in, he embraced me. The musk of that jacket was suffocating. He sniffled for a few seconds, then pulled himself away and rubbed his eyes.

"You...you're the best friend I've ever had, kid. You know that?" He choked and for a moment I was scared that he would actually break out into sobs. "Please just, you know, don't think of me badly." He was looking at his feet.

I awkwardly patted him on the shoulder. "Alright. Come on."

I helped him put his stuff into the truck again. As he got to the driver's seat, he suddenly let out this big, toothy smile.

"Last chance."

I waved him off. He shut the door, turned on the ignition, and I watched my truck and my plumber drive off. At the far end of the road they reached a bend, and, turning, they both were gone from my life forever.

For a second more I watched that bend, then, I pulled out my phone and ordered a taxi. Then, looking over at the other side of the road, I was surprised to see someone familiar watching me.

Katie was wearing a sundress of white and pink lilacs and leaning back on the hood of a car that Ben had his upper torso almost completely delved into. I had seen her wear it before. She was also wearing huge black sunglasses that covered almost half of her face and lazily biting something that looked like a toothpick. In the back window of their car I spotted a pile of suitcases. So they too were escaping some invisible thing, torn into the unknown by some irrepressible itch. I should've guessed it.

When she spotted me looking at her, she smiled and wiggled some fingers at me. She recognized me. I don't think she had any idea who Don was or even what I was doing there or what had just transpired. But she must have gathered by now that the blue truck parked outside of the bar was mine, and that I had just given it away.

And for some reason, at that moment, I felt as if I had missed out on the company of a fascinating and graceful person. We were both saying silent goodbyes - two strangers who did nothing more than drink and laugh and talk in the same room together.

Ben reappeared, closed the hood with a thud, and said something. He must not have seen me. Katie quickly glanced back and responded, opening the passenger door. Just before she got in, she flicked away the toothpick, took off her sunglasses, and looked over at me again.

She smiled - not sensually. Not mockingly. Not in pity. In warmth and acknowledgement of what could've been, of what was, and what would never be: a friendship missed out on. And most importantly of all, that she had accepted that, and she hoped that I would too. All communicated in the fraction of a single look in the setting sunlight on a desolate, miserable highway. I was in awe.

The door closed and separated us for good, and a moment later, the couple sped off in the same direction that Don had flown to. I sometimes wonder if they ever encountered one another - he on some journey of self-realization, and those two young, in love, and on their next adventure.

Life is too greedy with these quiet, incomprehensible moments. For that flash in time alone, I will never forget her.

<u>Chapter 15</u>

On a whim, I had the taxi take me to the beach near the Cliff House on the way home. I was too disjointed to go back to help Caesare, and I wanted to be near the ocean. I had him drop me off at the restaurant and walked down the hill to the dunes. There were a lot more people there this time around. Someone down a ways on the opposite end of the beach had set up a volleyball net, and some kids were wakeboarding a ways out near the isolated crags that guarded the shoreline. There was a group of people watching some older gentlemen flying elaborate, long kites that resembled dragons and spaceships in flight. I crossed through the short wall and glanced down to my left.

Lorelei's shoes were still huddled up in the sand, halfway melted into the ground. They were curled and rotted, and had lost all their color - the salt of the ocean had been blasting them for weeks. Bugs were swarming and crawling into and over them, and someone had desecrated them by shoving an empty beer bottle into one. I sat up on the wall and looked out into the Pacific. The last time I had been here the horizon was black and impenetrable: now it was alive with a sunset and almost inviting. The sea was golden, warm - the air thick with salt that had been carried across hundreds of miles just for me to breathe in.

I wondered where Don had decided to begin his journey, and what could have possibly happened, if anything, to make him completely uproot himself in so sudden a fashion. The one encounter I had had with his wife made them seem like the perfect match, or so I had thought. But I suppose no relationship exists without its troubles. Maybe it was the culmination of many small things. Maybe he'd been lying to himself all this time, maybe he really was having a midlife crisis and he would return, sheepish and ashamed. Did it even matter? The only change this made in my life was the loss of a conversation partner and that I'd have to find a new one at work.

That was what I told myself. In truth Don's sudden and dramatic exit, and my involuntary handing-off of my truck bothered me, tugged at me. He had seemed, out of everyone that I'd met here, the most stable and together. What did his disappearance mean for me, who had seen in him an authenticity I hadn't encountered before? How could he up and leave everything and everyone behind? It was uncharacteristically selfish.

I felt bad for Adelaide and her kids. They couldn't be called Don's anymore. He officially shirked that responsibility and the title of father. I wondered what they were going through now, and what they were going to do. I made a mental reminder to put a check in their mailbox. I had plenty of money and they were likely going to need some help, at least for now.

I just didn't understand it. It wasn't something a sane person would do. He had everything someone could've wanted, and his life was in complete control. What did he see, in some vague town up north, that he didn't here? What did he see that I couldn't?

"For weeks and months and years," I repeated to myself. It was impossible to know for sure. Some things just can't be put into words.

And as if the day had not had its fill of toying with my head, Elizabeth appeared out of the ether and sat down next to me just as the sun lightly kissed the edges of the water on the horizon.

I knew it was her immediately. Out of the corner of my eye her hair wisped and on the wind I caught her scent, awakening in some corner of my head visions of white hookah smoke and frenzied, drunken laughter, echoing off of mortar walls and bouncing directly into my nightmares.

Something primal awoke in me: the hairs on the back of my neck stood at full length, my heart suddenly felt tremendously heavy. I was frozen, and I couldn't even turn to look at her. But unquestionably, undeniably, this was *the* Elizabeth. How she had found me, where she had come from I couldn't even begin to guess, but my mind raced with possibilities until she laughed and confirmed her identity by that alone.

After situating herself, she spoke up. "You know, I heard you were in town." I couldn't move. I hadn't regained my composure or any sort of control over my words. She punched my shoulder, shattering what poise I had desperately started to accrue. "I can't believe this is how we run into each other. Do you live around here?"

Visions of the concert Lorelei and I had been to flashed in my head. Crowds of people in on the joke, the plot. Was she one of them, reclaiming her position from before? Did they surround us now? "No," I managed to get out. "Over n' Berkeley."

"Oh no kidding? I live right up the street, over there." She turned and pointed somewhere behind us. "Moved here about a month ago. I guess everyone's coming this way, I even heard that 3:16 was around. Isn't that weird?"

"Very strange."

"Man, it's been forever, hasn't it? When did you get out of jail?"

I wasn't hearing anyone behind us. My suspicion waned, but my attitude towards Elizabeth remained the same. "Long time ago. Wasn't in long."

"Yeah, my parents flipped and sent me to the fucking psych ward. Like a lunatic. I didn't know that I was sick, you know? I mean, they were obviously right, though. I hated them for it. I finished only a little while back."

"Oh!" She laughed and put her left hand in front of my eyes. "Look at that."

Pink nails. Cracked, dry skin between her fingers that blocked the sunset. A ring. An engagement ring. It was small, and instead of a diamond, her suitor had given her a ruby.

"Someone I met at the ward. His name's Andy. He's - incredible, really. A nice guy, I'll introduce you. Can you imagine?" She snorted with laughter and covered her mouth. "I can't believe I'm getting married. *Me*!"

For her misdeeds and crimes she was rehabilitated and sent back into society as a cured, pure soul. Accepted, and now, loved. If I did not hate her before, it was unquestionable now. Surprising visions of how to enact some incomprehensible revenge flitted through my head. In an instant, how she came here and how we ran into each other in a city the size of this no longer mattered.

"What about you?" She asked, breaking my spiral. "What have you been up to since then?"

I cleared my throat and tried to sit up straight. I refused to look at her. "I...uh, got a job. As a plumber."

"A *plumber*?"

"It pays the rent."

"I mean...yeah, you're right. Not like I'm any better. I don't have a job."

"Does Andy?"

"Yeah, he works for his dad or something. I don't know."

Out of the corner of my eye I caught a glimpse of her left hand again and realized why I had felt that something was off. The tattoo, 'Cigarettes Are Cool', her mark, was gone. It had been erased, and covered with a pink scar that could be explained off as a strange birthmark. My rage and disbelief for a moment got the best of me and I grabbed it, pulling her towards me.

"Hey, what -"

"What did you do to your tattoo?" I ran my fingers along the scars, like I was trying to find a gap in the skin to rip it off and reveal her shameful past to the world.

"You're crushing my hand, what's the matter with you?" The growing fear in her voice woke me up. I let her go and she quickly pulled away. My hands were shaking a bit, but I held onto my legs and controlled myself.

"I got it removed. It wasn't going to help me get a job or anything, you know. Being remembered for that."

"Yes, no, of course. You're right. I'm sorry, it was just - that, it was a thing we all recognized." I quickly tried to smooth it over. She relaxed a bit and placed her hand back down next to mine.

"Yeah. Well, you know. The past is the past."

The past is the past.

We watched the waves for a bit. Let the silence grow heavy. The wakeboarders were still throwing themselves into the darkening waters, but the volleyball game down the way had stopped.

How dare she erase everything as simply as that. Like she had never been involved. She might as well have gotten a new identity, a new face. A new life. How dare she be happy, find someone, and feel no guilt, no remorse? Not a word of apology to me, for everything that had happened? No, instead she got sympathy and stability. Everything she had pretended to stand for was gone and replaced with a sham to safely hide behind. I knew the real Elizabeth. We all did. A reckless sex addict who acted like the world owed her everything. In all of the daydreams and thoughts that I had experienced, imagining what a second meeting between myself and the person whom I blamed all of my misery on, I could not come up with a single word or action to make her feel a fraction of the same devastation I did. But I had to. I needed to. When was this opportunity going to present itself again?

"Well, it was great seeing you, okay?" She shifted as if to leave. My mind was racing so fast that I almost felt like a fever was coming on.

"If you're ever in the area, stop by. We'd love to-"

And then, suddenly, in a moment of terrible clarity, I knew what I could do.

I grabbed her hand, softly this time, and looked her directly in the eyes. She was wearing contacts to make them bright blue, and her features had become more pointed, more tired. Her cheeks, once so high and constantly smiling, were worn down. She was surprised. So was I. She had shed her senseless and careless exterior, sure, but this was still the same girl.

"Elizabeth," I smiled, "Where was it you said you lived?"

The ceiling fan looked down on me as if reproachful. Its ringing became a *tsk-tsk-tsk*.

I propped myself up on my elbows and glanced around the room, out of breath and eyes stinging with sweat. Elizabeth and Andy's den was decorated with movie posters and framed portraits of both families. It was dark outside now - the only window in the room was a small one right above the bed. Moonlight was streaming in to illuminate our feet.

She had her back turned to me. In the darkness I could make out some large tattoo starting from the base of her neck and dripping down her spine to her waist. She was shivering. I don't know if she was crying or just cold, but she was shaking. Bewildered. Angry. Good.

I could feel my blood pumping through my veins like oil, black and thick. My euphoria of exacting revenge came with a fleeting feeling of guilt that I tried to brush aside. This was what I had wanted, surely. Her confusion and regret were palpable in the musty, humid air.

I finally made a move to get up and get dressed. Who knew when her fiance would be arriving home, after all. I wondered whether or not she would be honest with him, tell him what had happened. Whether or not they could survive something like this. The guilt came back, but all I had to do was recall my jail time, dropping out of college, and all the frustration I had experienced since meeting her to make it all but disappear.

Without a word or a backwards glance, I reached the bedroom door and remembered something - a question that, if anyone would be able to answer, it would be her, and maybe only her. I looked back at black frame of the bed. Elizabeth's head was a wet mop of sweaty, curly hair.

"Do you know anything about what happened to Dead Richard?"

She immediately stopped shaking, and after a moment, very slowly, dramatically, pushed herself up. She brushed her hair behind her head and, in the small bit of light in that room, for a moment, her face was the only thing illuminated as she smiled sardonically, defiantly. Back to her old self. Obstinate, even in the face of total degradation. Equal parts admirable and infuriating.

"Last I heard," she mewed, "he was dead."

"Right." I sniffed. "Goodbye, Elizabeth." I turned and departed, determined never to see her again.

Chapter 16

Laugh, and the world laughs with you;

Weep, and you weep alone;

For the sad old earth must borrow its mirth,

But has trouble enough of its own.

Sing, and the hills will answer;

Sigh, it is lost on the air;

The echoes bound to a joyful sound,

But shrink from voicing care...

Leeroy's kick of depressing poetry choices had not let up, and there was no sign that it was going to anytime soon. It had been a few days since I had seen Don off into his own reckless adventures and ran into Elizabeth, and I had only just now left my apartment to see the status of things at the bar. Downstairs, the trio were playing another game of cards.

Walter glanced up at the sound of the door opening and nodded his head at me. The other two were too focused.

Ben and Katie's exodus left yet another tangible bullet hole in the place, and I felt bad for the Asian girl because now she was the only one who was consistently up on the second floor. She even looked relieved when I got my drink and took to my window seat. But she kept looking to their roosting spot, clearly becoming more and more concerned that they hadn't shown up yet.

I was annoyed that Elizabeth and Don were still on my mind. Earlier that day Adelaide had called my phone three or four times before giving up, which reminded me to put the check in her mailbox. Taking a cab all around the city wasn't cheap, but I figured I'd buy a used car or whatever sometime soon. I couldn't be bothered to look up a bus schedule. I didn't so much regret giving away the truck as I wish I understood why I'd done so. But Don, I was trying to reject and forget.

Seducing Elizabeth, I felt no qualms about. My only fear was running into her yet again. Regardless, both still were in my thoughts and I wanted to do something about that, so I decided to call up Arthur. Uncharacteristically, he picked up the phone barely through the first ring.

"Where the hell have you been?" I realized that we hadn't spoken since I returned to the state.

"Busy. You weren't worried about little old me, were you?"

"Well what happened with DuCard?"

"It went fine. I think. Haven't heard anything from them since."

"Well. That's good, then." Across the room, the Asian girl's drink went down the wrong pipe, and she started coughing hard.

"If you've got nothing to do today, you should stop by. I could use a hand with the gazebo."

"Gazebo?"

"Yeah, out back."

"That's what that space is turning into? A gazebo?"

"I'm just playing with the idea."

"It's hardly a gazebo, is it?"

"An altar, then."

"How much have you gotten done since I left?"

"I had to cut down some of the lower hanging branches from the trees that were getting in the way. But it'd be faster work if I had another hand."

"I'd stop by, but I don't have a car anymore."

"What happened to the truck?"

"I gave it away."

"You gave it away?"

"Yeah."

"What - what? Why? To who? When?" He sounded annoyed. Like this was a grave inconvenience to him.

"An acquaintance of mine needed it. A day or two ago."

"Well. That's...well." Now he was speechless. I couldn't blame him for thinking that was something I wouldn't do.

"Did you let him borrow it, or did you actually just give it away?"

"I probably won't be seeing him or the car again."

He was quiet for a second.

"I'd call a cab but I really don't want to spend the money to get to you."

"I guess I could give you a ride. Since you always make it up here on your own."

"I'd appreciate that. Do you know where I live?"

"No."

So I gave him my address and decided to walk back home. The Asian girl became visibly upset when she saw me leave her alone after only being there for around half an hour.

Arthur picked me up in an old station wagon at around 2:00, and smoking a cigarette. It was the first time I'd ever seen him smoke. I don't think he actually did habitually, but I didn't ask him about it. He was certainly coughing a lot, though. Halfway through the drive he awkwardly tried to put on some rock music, but got embarrassed partway through the first song and shut the radio off. He didn't ask any more details about my trip back home, which I appreciated.

We were about three blocks away from the church when he decided we were both hungry and passed through some drive in for lunch. He was about to pull away when he remembered something, and ran inside to pick up a small order for Brian. Only when we had parked did I notice the car about ten feet behind us.

Sitting in the driver's seat was Jenna, and next to her was Thomas. She was breathing heavily. Even from the rearview mirror I could make out her eyes - they were wide, red and unblinking, staring right back at me. Thomas was much calmer, but his mouth was moving, uttering something under his breath and fidgeting with something in his lap.

The sudden tension in the air jolted me awake into some sort of fight-or-flight. I glanced around the floor to see if there was any sort of weapon I could use, a gardening tool or something. No avail. I gently placed my foot over to the driver's side and on the brake, put the car in reverse, and slid my hand onto the bottom side of the steering wheel. I don't think they saw me. I could feel my forehead start to dampen as I began glancing from the doorway of the drive-in back to the rearview mirror. I had no idea when they started following us, or for how long.

When Arthur reemerged, things moved very fast.

As soon as he walked out, all four doors on the car behind me opened, and Thomas, Jenna, and two others that I had not seen and did not recognize jumped out. While Jenna and the other made a dash towards Arthur, I put the station wagon in reverse and drove it backwards, smashing the hood of the car and knocking Thomas and the other one over as they were getting out. The loud bang and car alarm startled the other two, who looked back and gave Arthur just enough wherewithal to realize what was happening, and dropping the food he fell into a sort of boxers stance. I got out and walked over to Thomas, who was struggling to get up. His forehead was bleeding - I guess the car door had thrown him pretty hard. Next to him on the ground was a small gun. I stared at it for a second, not fully believing it was there, then grabbed it and pointed it down at him, just as the other assailant in my peripheral vision lunged at me with a baseball bat. Instinctively I turned and fired the gun at him while his arms overhead prepared some barbarian swing.

It was a bb gun. Instead of a loud gunshot and flash of light, an embarrassing 'pop' echoed across the parking lot. But it hit him in the neck and he cried out, and staggered back a bit and grabbed his throat. I took the gun by the barrel and slammed it across his nose. Blood shot out and splattered onto the pavement while he reeled and stumbled to the ground. By this time Thomas had gotten up behind me, and full of adrenaline, I awkwardly threw a punch aimed at his jaw, which only barely connected but was enough to knock him back into the car.

I kicked the bat away and I looked over at Arthur to see how he was faring. One of the two was stumbling around holding his face in his hands, while Jenna, armed with what appeared to be some sort of rod, was swinging wildly at Arthur. His shirt was a little bloody but he was still standing on two legs. I was running over to them just as Jenna shrieked in frustration and lunged forward and smacked him, once on the forearm and once across the forehead as that arm fell. He crumpled, and as she bent down to rain more blows upon him, my right foot connected squarely with her cheek and launched her off. I quickly kneeled down to Arthur as she screamed in pain behind me. His forehead was bleeding and his eyes were closed.

"Arthur," I said loudly. "*Arthur.*" I looked up around us. People had started to stop, and a few had their phones out, recording.

"What the fuck did you - " the neckline of my shirt strangled me as someone pulled me from behind and threw me onto my back, knocking the wind out of me. Someone with a bloody mouth looked at me upside down from above, and spat in my face. "Motherfucker."

He was shaking a lot, and had to hold his left jacket pocket as his hand reached into it to grab something. I didn't want to know what that was, so I grabbed his leg standing next to my ear and pulled hard to the left, making him curse and stumble, but not hard enough to fall. I scrambled back up, and just as he pulled out what looked like a short knife I hit him with my left hand square in the nose. His head shot back but he cursed and used his free hand to try and wave me away. My right hand connected with his ear, hard, and he fell.

I turned back to Arthur. Jenna was at this point on her hands and knees, while underneath the car I could make out Thomas's feet as he crouched next to his friend, who was still on the ground.

Knowing that we were running out of time, I pulled Arthur up as gently as I could and lobbed back over to the car. As I struggled to get him back in, the thought occurred to me that this was not the first time that I had had to help someone back into the passenger's seat of a vehicle - while running from trouble, even. We managed to casually drive away just as police sirens were becoming audible. In the rearview mirror, Jenna was running over to the person I had knocked out. I couldn't see the other two. The whole thing had lasted maybe five minutes.

I only realized how badly my hands hurt as I was gripping the steering wheel on the way to the hospital - I thankfully knew where one was in the area since I'd driven past it on the way to church before. I painstakingly pulled my phone out of my pocket and dialed Father Brian as we drove.

"Hello! Good to hear - "

"We're on the way to the hospital. Nearest to you. Arthur's out cold. Can you make it there?"

He was quiet and started breathing quickly. The thought crossed my mind that I could be giving the man a heart attack.

"Brian. Can you make it there?"

"What happened?" His voice was sharper than I had ever heard it. I got the impression that somehow he was blaming me for this.

"Some kids jumped us. Somebody hit him in the head. Can you make it there?" He hung up.

"Hey..." My head shot to Arthur. He was stirring. Blood was now running in four rivulets down his face and dripping from his chin. One had crossed his left eye and when he blinked it became redder and redder.

"Did you...did you grab Brian's lunch?..." He was delirious. A police car in the opposite lane drove past us.

"Just put your head back. We're almost to the hospital." He closed his eyes again and nodded forward.

"What a day," he mumbled.

I pulled into the parking lot and quickly dragged him to the front door of urgent care. Somebody saw me carrying him in under my shoulder, and a few nurses ran out of the lobby and took him from me. Some others brought me inside and sat me down.

"Are you alright?"

"What happened?"

"Are you hurt?"

I tried to reassure everyone that I was perfectly fine, not only because I by some great luck was relatively unhurt, but I also had no insurance. I told them the truth about what happened, and the police were summoned. They arrived a little after Brian did, who burst into the lobby extremely flustered and wearing an old army coat over his frock. He rushed over to me and roughly grabbed me by my shoulders, which I really wished he wouldn't have.

"Are you alright? Where's Arthur?"

"I'm fine. They're taking care of Arthur in the back."

"How bad was he hurt?"

"He was sort of awake when they took him."

Just as he was about to ask again what had happened, the police came in. I carefully explained the circumstances to both parties. The two officers were large and a little annoyed, considering the fact that they were the ones who arrived on the scene just as I had left. I had a feeling that they were about to take me in myself, and I almost had flashbacks - had Brian, a priest, not been there to vouch for me.

I asked them what had happened to the people that attacked us, and one of them gruffly said that they had sped off just as the cops had arrived.

"Well did you catch them? We were just assaulted in broad daylight," I snapped. It had been a long day.

But thankfully they were patient with me. "We're working on it."

They departed after taking my information. A nurse soon came to Brian and I to be taken to Arthur, who had been spirited to a floor above us. She explained on the way that he had suffered mild blunt force trauma and a small fracture on his forearm. I thought that Brian was about to faint, and I suppose the nurse did as well, because she quickly added that "it was probably just a light concussion at worst."

His forehead had been cleaned up and stitches were already sewn into a rather small cut a few inches above his left eyebrow. He was awake now, but he looked tired.

As Brian fawned over his son I saw myself in a mirror hanging next to the bed and realized that I still had bloody spit dribbled over my face. I excused myself to the bathroom down the hallway.

As I washed myself off I suddenly felt exhausted, and physically dirty. I flexed my hands a few times under the dryer. They were extremely sore, and would be for about a week, but no bones were broken, as far as I could tell.

This had to be the end. Surely things could not progress any further than actually attacking myself and Arthur, out in the open no less, in full view. Having failed in whatever they were trying to do, so brashly, I couldn't imagine that they would try again - especially with the police now involved.

What even had they been trying to do, exactly? I don't know what they might have thought of us, but I never considered for a second that they would want to kill either Arthur or myself.

And the gun. It was a bb gun. If they really wanted to *kill* either of us, would it not have been a bit silly to try and do so with a toy? No, that wasn't their aim. It couldn't have been. I didn't know it was a toy, but they obviously did - so would they have tried to coerce us? Into the car, maybe? A kidnapping gone wrong? There was no way I could be sure, but it made sense.

Another thought was nagging at me which I was trying to ignore. I thought the gun was real. I tried to shoot one of them, and was disappointed. I chalked it up to an instinctual panic response, shook all of it off and walked back to Arthur's room. He was clearly coherent now, and getting angrier by the second, and was cursing and choking at the same time as the thought of how much this medical treatment was going to cost his father dawned upon him.

"I'm sorry, dad," I heard him sob as I walked back. I stood outside of the doorway. Brian hushed him.

"You're alright. That's all that matters."

"This shit, *again*. It happened *again*. I'm so *sorry*, God, I can't believe -"

Brian was quiet. "Arthur, Arthur. It's okay. Don't worry. We're going to be fine. Please just try and rest."

I decided that Arthur would never forgive me or himself if I saw him with tears rolling down his face, so I quietly skipped past them and made my way towards the exit. I was very tired now and really wanted to go home, and my plan was to call a cab straight back to Berkeley and fall asleep, for as long as possible. An older nurse stopped me as I was about to enter the stairwell.

"Excuse me, were you the one who drove that young man in room B22 here?"

"Yes. I've already given all of my information to the nurse at the front desk, and I myself am fine, so I'll be heading home now."

"Someone just stopped by looking for you. He said to give you this." She handed me a torn piece of paper. "Said it was urgent."

I took it and unfurled it. There were two strings of numbers and letters. I had no idea what to make of it, but after a moment it hit me - they were coordinates.

37°53'25.1"N 122°36'15.1"W

I was at a total loss. "I - I'm sorry, who gave this to you?"

"He didn't say his name. It was only a few minutes ago. The priest said you had just gone to the bathroom when I stopped by."

"What did he look like?"

"I'm surprised you didn't see him. We thought he was homeless at first, honestly. I mean, no offense or anything," she quickly apologized, "But we almost didn't let him in, until he mentioned you and the gentleman in B22 by name."

Something was very, very off. Cold had started prickling in my veins and blood suddenly rushed in my head - almost as if my body knew the answer to this question before I myself did. "What was he wearing?"

"That's the thing." She crossed her arms as if to defend herself from accusations. "I mean, the company you keep is your business, but you can't show up looking like that and expect people not to get a little suspicious. Makes our other patients uncomfortable." She sniffed.

"What was he wearing, miss?" My voice cracked with restraint. The paper she had given me was now crushed in a tight, white-knuckled fist.

Her brows furrowed. "I mean, a blue tracksuit jacket, a white hat, and of course the -" I didn't hear her finish her sentence. I was halfway down the stairwell and had burst out into the lobby within seconds. Every patron there looked at me funny as I scanned the room, panting. He wasn't there. I ran out the door and into the parking lot. Nothing. Cars floated by silently on the street, an ambulance lazily pulled into a stop close to me.

I ran farther. Down to the sidewalk, looking in every direction. Part of me wanted to scream his name, to announce his presence officially to myself and the world, but I knew it would be pointless. Dead Richard was gone.

Why had he decided to show up now? What was his connection to everything, and what did he want from me? I looked down at the coordinates again in the cab that drove me home. It had gotten late - street lights flickered on as we sat immobile in traffic, and the wind had started to pick up. There was likely going to be a storm tonight.

What a day. Part of me wanted to just throw the paper out of the window, to send it away into the darkness and rain and forget everything that had transpired, but I knew that I couldn't. Not now that Dead Richard was here. I folded it and placed it back in my pocket. When I finally made it home, I would only be awoken the next day by a call from Arthur in the late afternoon.

Chapter 17

"Where did you go?"

"I called a cab after they said you were going to be okay. Are you still at the hospital?"

"They discharged me this morning. Wanted to make sure it wasn't more serious than they thought, so they kept me overnight."

"And?"

"Just a small concussion. Apparently they go away on their own if they're minor enough. I got some stitches too. And pills."

"How's your head?"

"It looks worse than it feels. Thought my dad was gonna pass out."

"He almost did. At least he didn't see you before they cleared up all of the blood."

"Are you alright? I don't remember a lot after being hit."

"Somehow I managed to get out of it with only my hands hurting. I'll put them under ice. Should be fine."

"Yeah, I saw you. You got some pretty good punches in. Didn't you deck someone in the face with something?"

"A bb gun. I thought it was real."

"Okay, so it wasn't. I *thought* it looked like a gun."

"I think I broke his nose."

"Not like they didn't have it coming." A pause. "Did you recognize them?"

"Two of them. The girl and the one with the bb gun."

"I recognized the other two. They'd harassed me a bit sometime before you moved here."

"Is that right?"

"Small shit. They'd come to service and sometimes try to rile people up. Nothing this bad. How did you know the other two?"

"The guy I had run into a few times before. He plays in a band. I was introduced to the girl at one of his concerts. He knows who I was. I'm not sure if she does."

"'Was?'"

"Am. Who I am."

"Mm. What do you think they were trying to do?"

"They couldn't have actually been trying to kill us. A fake gun wouldn't do that."

"What, then? Why?"

"I was trying to figure that out...kidnapping, maybe? I don't know. But I think we won't see them again."

"What makes you so sure?"

"That they failed miserably and the police got involved. Doesn't mean I'm not going to be careful, though."

"Yeah. Yeah, alright. I don't know."

I hesitated telling him about the note, but I decided it was better to be honest about any communications I'd received from anyone we both knew - especially in the case of Dead Richard, who I always thought only a few people knew of anyways. "Listen, I, uh..as I was leaving last night, someone gave me something. A nurse. She said someone had come by and mentioned us both by name."

"What, you and me? What'd they give her?"

"It was just a note. With some, uh, coordinates on it."

"...okay? Who from?"

"Here's the thing," I held my breath. "She described someone who looked a lot like Dead Richard."

"What the *fuck* -" he hissed into the receiver. Whether it was out of spite or because he was trying to hide his language from Brian I wasn't sure.

"I know."

The sound of something clattering in the background indicated that he was moving around. I pictured him pacing back and forth in the church kitchen. "Where - when did he get here? How did - "

"I don't know. I tried to chase him outside, but he was gone."

"Coordinates. You said coordinates. You didn't look up where those coordinates were, did you?"

"Well no, not yet. But I feel obligated to."

"Don't. Are you insane? Do you remember him at all?" He interrupted me before I could say anything. "How did he know we were at the hospital? What if he's behind that hit?"

I hadn't considered that. This was not impossible, but I couldn't think of any feasible reason why Dead Richard would want to do harm to either Arthur or myself. Or why he'd want people to kidnap us - and even if he did, I really did not see Richard as ever doing anything but alone. How he knew we were at the hospital, I couldn't explain.

"I don't know about that. And what did you have against him to begin with?"

"Are you serious? He's a freak. There's something wrong with him, and he's dangerous," He huffed. "He's a legitimately crazy person, he's unstable and *deranged*. And they *worshiped* him back there. Those are the same people who put me in a hospital. Twice now."

"Look-"

"*Twice.*" He swore again, loudly this time. I guess Brian wasn't around. "I can't believe he's here now. Of *course* he's mixed up in all of this."

"I get it. But Richard...he never came off like - like he'd be responsible for anything like that. To me at least. I'm just not convinced. We have no idea what he could want."

"'We?'" he snorted obnoxiously. "This is all on you. Leave me out of this. I want nothing to do with him, and whatever you do is your business, but if you've got a brain cell left in your head you'll tear up that note and wash it down the drain."

"Look." I rubbed my eyes. He was beginning to give me a headache. "I'll let you know what I decide to do. Okay?" He cursed to himself again and hung up.

I mulled over the whole matter for about a whole week. I worked with Caesare again, who made no mention of Don or his disappearance, but nodded in approval at my banged up hands.

"*Ben fatto,*" he chuckled as I was wiping off some grease. He pointed at my knuckles with a hairy, gnarled finger of his own. "Securing the honor of some, ah, *pretty girl*, yeah?"

"If only. My friend and I were jumped." His laughing face suddenly dropped and he became serious.

"They jumped you? Like from a car?" He made as if to drive a steering wheel to make sure I understood.

"Yes, exactly."

"*Criminali*? Ah, ah, gangsters?"

"No, nothing like that. It's hard to explain."

"But you fought them off, ah? That is what matters." He smiled again.

"I guess so." He chuckled and turned around back to work.

"Good. Maybe now you won't have trouble, when people hear you can fight."

That night I headed to the bar on one of those rent-a-bikes and encountered a large, yellow notice of impending foreclosure and subsequent demolition posted on the front door. The date it gave was in the next week, but promised that they would be open up until the very last minute. I assume that Leeroy finally felt that it was too much to bear, working the same job his disappeared girlfriend did at an establishment they had run together. I wasn't so much upset as I was furious that he felt like he could do this without my consent. Empty of sympathy at this point, I tore it off and stormed inside. The three were in the back of the room laughing and talking loudly about something, and only stopped to look up as Leeroy shouted at me before I could shout at him.

"*There* you are," he snapped, standing up from his stool at the end of the bar and throwing his magazine down. I made it to the bar and had opened my mouth to hurl some insult at him when I lost all air.

"Some guy has been coming by asking about you. Like, a lot. I don't know what your deal is, but if you've got trouble you keep it away from here. Alright?"

I realized that after a moment that my mouth was still open.

"I - uh, ah, are you sure they were asking for me?"

"He didn't mean anyone else who comes here regularly. Said he wanted to talk to you about a mutual friend."

My mind was quickly going through what new and old acquaintances I had made, and which of them knew one another.

"What did he look like?"

"Black guy. Brown coat, short hair. Carried a trash bag on his shoulder. I thought he was homeless." I knew nobody of this description.

"They weren't looking for me. They wanted somebody - "

"He said you'd recognize the name Richard. Look, just stop by tomorrow at noon or whenever you get the chance. He's come by every day looking for you and it's been really annoying."

I blinked and cleared my throat. "Did he say anything else?"

"Nope. Wouldn't buy a drink so I had to kick him out."

"I see. Well. Thank you." I very stiffly turned and walked back the way I came, feeling the eyes of everyone there boring holes into my spine.

I returned home and looked up the coordinates I'd been given the night before. I was not sure what I was hoping for or expecting, maybe a building downtown or at least something easily reachable or at least in public. This was not the case.

They landed on the far western end of Mt. Tamalpais national park, a good distance from any roads or buildings and near the coast. It was so far removed from anything that I thought it had to have been located in a restricted area of the reserve. This really didn't make anything easier for me.

I wondered again who this person was that had come by asking for me at the bar. He may have been associated with Thomas and Jenna, and after they failed to coerce us (or do whatever it was they planned to do), maybe they had sent someone after us individually. I called Arthur to ask if he had encountered anyone of his description.

"Not in the least. A trash bag?"

"That's what he told me."

"And he asked about Dead Richard?"

"Yeah, but didn't say anything else about it. He's come by asking for me every day."

"...How often do you go to this bar for someone to reasonably assume that you might be there on any given day?"

"Oh. Uh, often enough, I guess." I hadn't realized until now that Arthur had never been to the bar. He probably wouldn't have liked it.

"Will someone else be there when you're with him, if you meet him?"

"There's usually one or two people around."

"So if he wanted to try something, someone would be there to step in."

"Maybe. He might just be looking for Richard, and think that I would know where he is."

"What makes you think that?"

"Just a hunch."

"Speaking of Richard. Those coordinates. Did you -"

"Yes, in the middle of nowhere. Far edge of Mt. Tamalpais Park."

"The...national park?"

"Looked like it."

"It's not like you're backed into a corner, but if I were you I'd just give this guy what he wants and be done with it. If he does end up asking what you know about Richard."

"Let's see what he has to say. I can't be sure until I meet him."

"You're going to go, then?"

"If he's been there every day looking for me, chances are I'll run into him one way or another anyways."

"You could just, you know, start going to a different bar." This was simply not an option, but I couldn't explain that to him.

The next day was blistery and sunny, with the bay choppy and the seagulls blown every direction far above as I made my way back. I took a deep breath and opened the door, having no idea what to expect.

The tide rises, the tide falls,
The twilight darkens, the curlew calls;
Along the sea-sands damp and brown
The traveler hastens toward the town,
And the tide rises, the tide falls...

Purple wisps of smoke were dripping in thin tendrils from beneath the floorboards above in the bar. Whoever he was, he was waiting for me upstairs. The entire place reeked of a pungent smell that brought me all the way to the basements and dirty carpets of back home:

Hookah. It singes your nose hairs and makes your eyes stream if you're around the smoke too long. Synthetic flavors creep into your mouth and stick in the back of your throat just by being in the same room, and dirty, smoky water stains the ceiling and billows out in huge, cancerous clouds.

The Asian girl had been forced from her spot by the odorous stench, and was sitting where I usually did on the first floor, over near the large window, typing away furiously, clearly livid about this unprecedented change in protocol. I went to Leeroy, who handed me my drink on the grounds that this stranger be out of here in an hour's time, or he would kick *both* of us out, and went upstairs.

The entire second floor was smog pierced by rays of sunshine. I don't know how long he had been waiting for me, but I could barely make out in the back corner of the room the silhouette of a figure sitting before a small hookah. I waved the smoke out of my face and trudged forward to meet whoever this was. He made no movement and only acknowledged me by following me with his eyes through the smoke as I sat down opposite of him.

We both simply sat there for a moment. He was wearing a big beige trucker hat with some logo on it I couldn't quite make out, a brown jacket with a plain white shirt, and on the floor next to him, sure enough, was a white garbage bag filled with possessions. But in the smoke I could see his eyes clearly. Angry, about something. Piercing and bright.

He took a long drag off of his pipe and blew a stream out of the corner of his mouth and away from me.

"Sorry, can you knock it off? It stinks in here. And you're not supposed to smoke," I added, as if that was going to be what stopped him. His eyes widened in indignation, like he was offended - but he put down the straw and covered up the coal.

"Thank you. Now what do you want?"

He just kept his eyes on me. Despite how mad he looked, he was relaxed, his legs crossed and nonchalantly leaning back in his chair, as if he hadn't been trying to meet with me for days and this was just a chance occurrence.

"Fortunato," he exhaled a last stream of smoke through his nose, "You're harder to find than I thought." His voice was clear and deep. I suspected it would be raspier, if he smoked hookah regularly.

"I didn't know people were looking."

"You must've had some idea."

"Maybe a bit." He looked back up.

"Why all the hiding?"

I shook my head. "That's a stupid question. I was assaulted the other day by people who *had* been looking for me. I'm guessing you're here about that."

"No. Not at all."

"You're not?"

"No. I'm alone. It sounds like you have a lot of people after you."

"You don't know anyone named Thomas and Jenna?"

"No, I don't."

"So what's your deal, then? Is this about the riots? Because if it is, please, do not waste my time. There's nothing more to talk about."

"It is, in a sense. But it's more about the people involved. One person in particular." His eyes narrowed.

"So I was told. Why are you looking for him?"

He let out a deep sigh that blew the clouds away from him momentarily. My question must've been impertinent. Downstairs I heard Leeroy swear once, loudly, at the ceiling. I imagine for the smoke still settling through the floorboards.

"Let me ask you this," he said. "How well do you remember him?"

"He's not easy to forget."

"Especially considering that you two were so closely associated."

"Now hold on," I put up a finger. "Let me be clear. We weren't friends. We were just in the same place at the same time."

"I never said you were. But you both did hold a special spot, didn't you? You and that girl."

"Against our will."

He looked directly into my eyes. They were sharp, even in the shadows. Every word I said was being measured. "All of your will, or just *yours*?"

"Mine, at least. I don't know where he is. We haven't kept in contact."

He kept giving me his suspicious, judgmental glare. Outside the wind had died down.

"What do you want from him, anyway? What's your deal?"

"I've been looking for Dead Richard for a long time."

"How long is a long time?"

"Since those riots ended."

I felt myself physically recoil in my chair. "You've followed him - you've been looking for him since *then*?"

"Yes."

"Are you serious?"

"Yes."

"So you're obsessed. It's no wonder the bartender thought you were insane. Did you go to school there? Were you in the riots?" He frowned.

"No and no."

"What on Earth led you to hunting him down to here?"

The smoke had begun to dissipate and I could discern his features; a flat nose and a sharp chin. He looked weather-worn, and he had veiny, purple bags under his eyes. I could see now that his brown coat was dirty, and had been sewn back together above the left shoulder. Physically, he looked well built but drained of energy - maybe he really had been following Dead Richard all of this time. Under the brim of his hat poked out short thick vines of curled, black hair. I could make out the logo which read, in a huge box,

The Apple Barn Applewood Farm, with a banner between labeled *Cider Mill And General Store*.

"He is dangerous. In every sense. The riots ended, but Richard did not stop there."

"Stop what? He wasn't violent. I only ever saw him react to people trying to hurt him."

"I have seen it. In the sleeve of his right forearm he hides a switchblade, and I have seen him use it. But you are right - I don't refer to his violence. Were he just some crazy kid with a knife I would not be here." He folded his hands and leaned forward.

"It is his apathy. Apathy towards your fellow man, apathy towards the world around you and the events in it. Apathy towards everything and anything but yourself and what you desire," he leaned in a little further. "And people *listen* to him," he whispered.

I let that sit in the air for a second.

"What he *promotes* is dangerous to you? That he's some kind of, what, a nihilist?"

"He is poisonous. A libertine with an agenda. He advocates a life spent wandering. A useless life, without responsibility or value. And what's worse is that he has an audience." His entire frame began to inflate with emotion. His hands, even clasped as they were, started to shake.

He was barely able to keep his voice calm. "It is attractive because people do not want responsibility or to work. Those riots secured his martyrdom and now new followers spring up in his wake. I have seen them and met with them. They are fanatics."

I was bewildered. Out of every single way I could have imagined this conversation with this stranger to go, this absolutely was not one of them. "You've been tracking down a homeless person for something like seven or eight months because some kids decided to try and turn him into a cultural icon? About being *lazy*? Do you have any idea how insane you sound?"

His hands were so tightly holding one another that they had started to pale. "It is more than that. Richard himself..." he trailed off, shaking his head and looking out the window. "Richard...there's something wrong with him. Something unnatural, and dangerous, and constrained to him alone."

"What're you talking abo-"

"Things," he rolled his eyes back to me and let out an exacerbated huff, "*happen* around him. Things that just shouldn't happen. I don't know what it is, but it's there. You have not seen him since the riots. He's changed. He is more dangerous than you remember."

We let the silence hang for a few moments as he regained his composure. He was so close to being overwhelmed with anger that I was on the verge of taking off if he had lost control. He eventually leaned back and relaxed himself.

"You haven't seen him since the riots ended, correct?" He was watching the bay now, back in control of himself.

"That's right."

"And no contact at all?"

"None."

"Are you lying to me?"

"Yes." He looked back at me and smiled.

"Then why don't you tell me what you know? You don't have any reason to protect him."

I paused. "It sounds to me like you're someone he'd need to be protected from."

He just looked at me, then went back to watching the water.

"You think he's just a drifter," he stated quietly. "A dangerous one, maybe, but just a loner. But he's more than that."

"To you, maybe."

"His influence is greater than you know or want to believe."

A scary thought suddenly occurred to me. "Are you hunting down Elizabeth and I as well?"

"Don't get me wrong. I'm not a fan of either of you. But you're not nearly as threatening." Suddenly I guess he was inspired, and looked up at the ceiling. "You were in the right place at the right time, really. After all, what hope does a falling leaf have of making an impression on the ground below it, unless it manages to land on wet cement?"

"Glad to hear it."

"How long has she been in the city?"

"Who knows. Everyone seems to turn up here."

The smoke had almost completely gone by now. Sunlight was streaming through the last few clouds and particles left behind in the air.

"So," he sighed again. Greasy, empty shadows moved all over him. "You're not going to tell me anything."

"I'm afraid I am not."

"Do you plan on seeing him?"

"That...I haven't decided."

"Well," he made the motion to gather himself, as if it took every last bit of energy he had, and, grabbing his trash bag, he tied the hookah up and stuffed it in. "Be careful if you do. I'll find him whether or not you help me."

"Any message you want me to deliver?" I asked, half mocking.

"Don't bother. There's nothing to communicate between us."

He tied the string up and shouldered the bag like it was a knapsack. As he turned to depart, I only then recognized what appeared to be the hilt of a large knife peeking out of the small opening at the top.

He got to the stairwell and stopped. Without looking back, he said

"You know, Fortunato, you two are more similar than you probably like to think."

He didn't wait for a reply, as if I had one to give. He walked downstairs and I heard the front door slam a second later, which was then immediately followed by a faint "finally!" from below.

Chapter 18

"You didn't even get his *name?*"

Arthur called my phone as I was on a job with Caesare. We were doing some outside work, actually not too far from where I lived, on the marina. I had had my meeting with Dead Richard's pursuer a day ago. Caesare angrily waved me off as I apologized, stepping aside to take the call.

"No, I didn't. Our conversation didn't last very long."

"Did you learn anything about him?"

"Only that he really, really does not like Dead Richard."

"So he's sane." I kicked away a seagull that had hopped over to me, anticipating that I was going to toss some bread crumbs.

"Wouldn't go that far. He also carries around a trash bag with what looks like a huge knife in it."

Arthur was silent for a moment. "What is it about you that attracts these types of people?"

"Buddy, I wish I could tell you."

"Anything else?"

"He smoked a hookah and didn't get angry at me when I told him that I wasn't going to give up Richard's whereabouts."

"A hookah?" Another pause. "Do you think he might have anything to do with the people back-"

"I thought the same thing, but I don't think so. He didn't give any indication that he was involved."

"And you really think that Richard's in the middle of a national park?"

"I wouldn't be surprised."

"This is a completely normal line of thinking."

"It's Richard, you know. I wouldn't put it past him." Another thing occurred to me. "This person...also seemed to indicate that there was something off about Richard."

"Well, yeah. No shit."

"No, more than that. He said that things 'happen around him'."

"Meaning?"

"I have no idea. He didn't go any further."

The sound of metal clanking from behind indicated that Caesare was taking his frustration with me out on whatever we were supposed to be accomplishing.

"Listen, I think I'm going to go see him."

"You're making a huge mistake."

"I want you to take me."

"No. Absolutely not. No."

"Arthu-"

"No."

"I'm not asking you to go see him. I just need a ride to the park. I still don't have a car."

"Well, whose fault is that?"

"I'm asking you for a favor. Please. I really don't want to go alone."

The last bit came out on accident, and I was suddenly a bit embarrassed. It was the truth, though: while I really did not believe that Dead Richard would be of any danger to me, the prospect of going to face him alone, especially in the middle of nowhere, made me uncomfortable. If Arthur couldn't stand to meet with him, maybe he could at least accompany me to his doorstep.

What was even more humiliating was that Arthur caught a hint of my anxiety. He cursed to himself quietly, and then a bit more loudly.

"When were you planning on going?"

"The sooner the better. Tomorrow work for you?"

"Fine. I'll give you a ride."

"Thank you. Seriously."

"Might as well see this thing through, I guess." he grumbled.

That night I looked up the location again, just to make totally sure I hadn't fat-fingered the coordinates one more time. It was almost right next to Lone Tree Creek, and actually, there was a dirt road which turned into a walking path a relatively short distance away from it. It was still far out of the way for the main part of the reserve, but the prospect of not having to hike forever was a relief. We would have to drive about an hour to get there.

Arthur showed up the next day early in the morning, but not looking too worse for the wear. The trophies he earned from our fight not a week before were still recovering, his stitches on his temple black and blue and his left eye adorned with a curved bruise like some child had haphazardly taken a marker and tried to draw glasses on him. He was still wearing his clerical collar - there must've been an early morning service held today. His eyebrows shot up when I got in.

"What?"

"It's - I mean - look at the state of you." I looked up and down myself.

"I'm fine."

"Exactly. Now look at me." He gestured to his face. "How is that fair?"

He laughed. A dry and forced thing. We turned and sped off to try and beat the morning traffic. This of course did not happen, and we ended up being stuck on the Golden Gate bridge.

"Last chance to change your mind, by the way," Arthur remarked as he rolled down a window. It was clear and bright outside. Fog was rolling off of the water below and through it you could make out the twinkling lights of lampposts on the pier, on the verge of ending their night shifts.

"You're not the least bit interested in finding out what his deal is, are you?"

"Not at all."

"He's not at fault for what happened to you back home. Or recently."

"How could you know?" He sniffed. "You know just as much about him as I do."

"Isn't it better to find out for sure?"

"If he ends up wearing your skin like Buffalo Bill, I told you so."

"There's got to be a reason why he reached out to us. Nobody's seen him in a long time, I think."

The traffic suddenly lifted. The roads dipped and curved in a smooth route for the rest of the way out of the city, and then we were on a few roads left before we would arrive at the entrance to the park. It was warm out, and the wind billowed through the car carrying with it now the salt of the ocean. The roads soon turned from dipping through hills to skating along their faces. We were getting closer: thin trees poking out of craggy, rough ground turned and bent in the wind. Soon, we were the only car on a secluded road, about a mile out.

"Do you even know if he'll be there?"

"He'll be there."

"How do you know?"

"He has to be."

He glanced over at me and didn't say anything else. Soon we passed back into woodland and reached a large, wooden arch signifying our arrival at the park. The lot was sparse - it was a weekday, no not crowded with visitors. I got out to ask the attendant for directions to Veterans Bench, the closest landmark to where Richard's coordinates had landed. When I got back to the car, Arthur had gotten out and was staring at a notice board nearby. He gestured me over without looking away.

"Look at this shit."

The board was covered with what appeared to be hazy surveillance camera photographs and sketched drawings of a man in an animal mask. In most of the photos, he was a blur, rummaging through trash cans or barely perceivable past the trees.

One clear photo was at the center, and had been shot at the reception pavilion I had just walked from. Taken from above, Richard's face was barely perceptible in the darkness, but you could tell that he was looking directly into the camera. All you could see was the mask and his hat - and the thin outline of his shoulders, and below him a bit further, the ghost of a torn-up gloved hand. His eyes remained hidden, and did not reflect any bright light as was usually the case in these types of infrared photographs.

No emotion betrayed. No thoughts revealed. Empty, soulless and ridiculous.

The sketches which accompanied the photos were only of his masked face and hat. It was incredibly unnerving to see him depicted anywhere, in any context, after only having had fuzzy memories of him: his costume had remained entirely unchanged after all this time. The only thing I noticed was a large crack that some drawings showed in his disguise, stretching from the top right of his face through his right eye and into the snout.

A sign above all of this asked "HAVE YOU SEEN THIS MAN?" and "DO NOT APPROACH".

"Excuse me," I called out to a park ranger who was walking by. "What's the deal with this?"

She came over smiling, but her face quickly clouded when she looked at the board. "We've had sightings of this person in restricted areas and at closed hours. A few visitors have reported spotting him, too."

"How long has this been going on?"

"Only about a month. Please don't be too worried. The people who have seen him have all reported that he runs away if he's noticed. We don't think he's dangerous, but his appearance has, ah, you know, caused a bit of a stir." She giggled awkwardly. When neither Arthur nor I returned a laugh, she sobered up. "He is trespassing on federal grounds, and we do take it very seriously. Have you seen him yourselves?"

"Us? No. We just got here."

"Well, *please* don't let this spoil your day trip! Which way are you two headed?" She quickly changed the subject. After I had given her some story about what trails we were looking to hike, she left, and I turned back to Arthur. He was still staring at the photos.

"You alright?" I asked. He was squinting, looking back and forth between the sketches and the photographs.

"Did he always have that big gash on his mask?" He nodded towards one of the drawings.

"No, I don't think so."

"I can't believe he never got rid of that. You never saw him without it on, did you?" He looked back at me.

"No. He never took it off."

He shook his head in disbelief and glued his eyes back to the board, scanning for something, or trying to convince himself that he was really there.

"It's weird...seeing him again." He finally managed to get out.

I looked back at the photo of him staring into the camera. In the darkness, he was alone, as if a spotlight had singled his shadow out. Only the corner of a nearby dumpster was visible to his far right. So familiar, yet so alien. After having known him for as long as we both did, neither of us could imagine what his life had been like since we had all parted ways. What had gone through his mind. He was still a stranger to the both of us.

"Come on," I patted Arthur's shoulder. "Let's go find him."

Veteran's Bench was secluded and far removed from the nucleus of the park, where most visitors stayed. To get to it, you had to meander on a road that went straight from gravel to dirt, and the farther you got out, the more unkempt even that became. Eventually we pulled out of the dense redwood forest and onto empty fields, towards the park's perimeter. The end of the road disappeared into windswept dried grass and brown rock. As Arthur pulled to a stop, he tossed something into my lap, wrapped in brown paper.

"What's this?"

"Just in case." I unwrapped it. It was a large bowie knife, the leather sheath of which was so aged that it had started to green and peel.

I picked it up and weighed it in my hand. It was heavy, almost like a machete. "Are you serious? Look at this thing."

"It's my dads. He doesn't know I took it."

"Well, thanks. But I don't need it." I put it on the seat as I got out of the car. He leaned across and looked up at me through the window.

"How long do you think you'll be?"

I didn't hear him. I was looking around us. The hills were visible for miles and miles away, rolling over one another and bulging like brown and green muscles out of the Earth and covered with the ghosts of morning mist. There was nobody else out here, and all you could hear was the wind, the birds - and the ocean, which to the West and below expanded into the horizon in a thick, white line at some parts, and at other points so blue that the ocean and the sky seemed to meld into one.

I turned and looked down the pathway which was to lead me to Richard. There were no fresh footsteps, but animal tracks. Some pointed paw prints with claws, more hooves, blending together. Further down a ways, it turned into the underbrush which led back into the woods.

"Hello?"

"I'll try to be brief."

I stood there looking down the path for a bit, thinking about my upcoming meeting, when I realized that Arthur was still watching me.

"You're nervous." I could hear him smiling. Why he was laughing I had no idea.

"Of course I'm nervous."

"Then take the knife."

"I'm not nervous about that."

"What, then?"

"I don't know. Where are you going to wait?"

"There was a campsite about a mile back. I'll just hang around there."

"Okay."

I felt his eyes on me still, but he finally muttered something sounding like "good luck, I guess," and he rolled up the window and backed up. I heard the car pull away slowly, like he was watching me in his rearview mirror, and then fade off, leaving nothing but the sounds around me and the path forward, leading, it seemed, into the skyline itself.

<u>Chapter 19</u>

Because of the elevation, and the sloping hills down towards the ocean, the wind blew up and across the plains with particular force. It threatened to push me off of the path and summoned small tornadoes to cross me as I meandered through the grass and stumbled over the rocks. I knew from looking up the coordinates that this pathway was yet not secluded, not secret enough for Richard to be hidden from. I kept my eyes peeled for the final stretch of dirt that would jut away from this one and take me towards the treeline to the North, which stood, parallel and imposing, to my walk. I glanced around me once again to either make sure I was alone, or to dreadfully confirm it. No one could be seen. The only animals visible were birds - falcons - small and wild, fighting the rough winds high above.

Finally I saw a small, thin ghost of a pathway perpendicular to the one I had been trudging on. I stopped and looked down it. The wind was ferocious: my eyes squinted in the dust that was being thrown in great gusts all around me to try and make out where this new road led. There was nothing to be discerned from the stoic line of redwoods towering out of the ravine which the path stopped at. The trees, so incredibly vast and ancient, bulwarked against the wind with only the faintest fluttering visible from the highest points of their branches, waving almost as if in stuffy formality rather than being forced against their will. More out of a desire to be shielded from the wind than in a haste to find Dead Richard, I scampered my way down to the end of the walkway, bounded through the first fifteen or twenty feet of wild, unkempt grass, and broke into the woods.

One thing I did not know, and learned only some time later, is that redwood trees are unique in that their bark is particularly thick, and their foliage is such that only the most adventurous birds or squirrels would seek to climb the enormous distance from the ground to the nearest branch, which precariously bends hundreds of feet above. As it was, all sound was muffled or completely absent as soon as I stepped into the forest. No winds blew past me, no birds screamed in the air or squirrels leapt into the underbrush. No insects buzzed. Even the thunderous crashing of the ocean, before distant but audible, was completely erased. The only sound was my own breathing, admittedly troubled, and my steps, marked with trepidation.

I knew that the location marked had landed very close to the stream that flowed through this part of the reserve, Lone Tree Creek, and that I would eventually find the stream itself if I continued forward. What made this so much more difficult was that this was an unkempt part of the territory - there was no dirt trail to follow, and roots and rocks jutted out of the ground and pushed the earth into uneven mounds and twists. I stumbled more times than I could count, but just as I was beginning to lose my patience the soft sound of running water reached me. Past a few more colossal trunks I found the creek. I turned south and walked along the stream, which almost silently glided over the grass and through the dirt in an undisturbed zig-zag pattern - bubbling under fallen trees and coursing through small banks of clay, I finally reached what had to be what was Dead Richard's hideaway. At this point I was at least a few miles from where I had departed from Arthur.

Thirty or so feet away from the water, after walking along it for around twenty minutes, the cubed shape of an ancient shack appeared, hidden away and tucked behind the trees. The wood it was made from was rotting, the moss which enveloped it spreading from the shoddy boards and seeping into the land at its base. It was very small, perhaps eight feet by twelve, and it had clearly been standing here for a very long time: part of the front corner had collapsed, and it seemed so frail that I worried about it falling down on me if I were to make any sort of sudden movement inside. There were no windows, or holes for windows. There was a door made of some newer wood - you could tell because it was at least a fraction brighter than the rest of the tiny abode, and not touched by rot - and facing this I stood, trying to catch my breath. Not from walking all of this distance, but in preparation of finally meeting him.

Finally, I put my hand up to the door and knocked, resulting in a dull, thick sound. It seemed silly to go through with such formalities for so wild a home, in so remote a place, but who knows what he might've done had I walked in unannounced? Dead Richard likely knew that the forest rangers had been looking for him, and I remembered the warning that had been passed to me from the man with the knife about how dangerous Richard, apparently, was.

But no one responded. I knocked again, harder. Nothing. Maybe he was out and about - scavenging, or whatever he did for food. I called out to him.

"Richard? Are you in there?" My voice sounded so small underneath the huge trees, and I felt that I had broken some rule by interrupting the blissful silence here. He had to have heard me now. There was no other sound around to cover me up. But still, no response. I gently opened the door. If he was out, then he would find me waiting for him here.

This was not the case. I opened the door fully, and only from the light behind me did I make out his silhouette, sitting behind a makeshift table made of a rusty car door, with his mask partially up off of his face and his hands eating something. It looked like a bag of chips. How I hadn't heard that through the door is beyond me. My heart must have been pounding too loudly, my ears too flushed with blood. Hanging, dangling from the rotting wood above were long green strands of moss, almost touching his shoulders.

I stood, frozen, watching him. He just sat there and continued to eat, his filthy, gloved hands lazily grabbing handfuls and shoving it into his mouth. Though his mask had to have been at least partially up off of his face, I could make no features out. He was bowed forward a little bit, hiding himself from me. I had forgotten how frail, how thin he was. And for the first time, he wasn't wearing that coat. A dirty white t-shirt hung on his frame, and the only skin I have ever seen of him was that of his arms. They were so pale that they were almost translucent. If at any point beforehand I had doubted whether or not this person was THE Dead Richard, if I wondered if someone had maybe commandeered a very convincing lookalike outfit, this put those doubts completely out of my mind. There was simply no one else that sickly, that lanky.

"Richard?" My voice thankfully didn't crack from fear. My throat had started to swell up. He made a slow sweeping motion with his arm, like he barely had the strength in him to do so, and gestured me to come inside. I stepped in, closed the door behind me, and slowly sat across from him on an uprooted stump.

He continued to eat until the bag was empty. Then he crumpled it up, and pulled his ridiculous otter mask fully back down over his face - a long scar dragged across the forehead down to the nose, like it had looked in the surveillance photos at the park's entrance, and his eyes were still covered by something behind the mask. He just sat there, contemplating me for a second, then stood up with great effort and walked back into the corner behind him, where I could make out his jacket lying on the ground next to a sleeping bag. He crouched down, rifled through something, and brought back a canteen to the table. He offered it to me.

"Is it water?" I asked. He nodded, removed the cap and handed it to me.

"Thank you." He watched me as I drank in a few gulps. Surely he would need this more than I would, so I didn't want to be greedy. He sat down opposite from me and tossed it back into the corner when I had finished.

We simply sat there for several long, quiet moments. I had no idea what to say. When I finally opened my mouth to ask him how he came to be here, he spoke.

"It is good to see you again, Fortunato."

Underneath his mask he was using some device to disguise his voice. It was deep and guttural, and betrayed nothing of his natural intonation. I had never heard him speak before, with or without that thing on. In the silence of that place, and in the confined wooden walls, he was very loud. His words flew out of him like some blast of wind and noise, and I was so taken aback and thrown off that I had to grasp for words.

"I-uh- yeah, yes. You too, Richard."

"Was it a long journey?"

"No. Not too long, no. There's a public road that brought me pretty close to here."

"Mmm. Did you drive yourself?"

"No, Arthur brought me."

"Mr. 3:16. I take it he did not wish to meet with me."

"He did not."

He nodded. **"That is probably for the best."**

I hesitated. "He's convinced that you're going to, uh, try to hurt me."

He waved his hand as if the mere thought was a pestering fly in the air. **"An entirely foolish notion. But then again he and I were not as well acquainted as we are."**

Were we acquainted at all? That he felt some sense of closeness to me, and after all of this time, came as an unexpected surprise. How it came about in the first place I had not the slightest idea.

He looked me up and down. **"Have you heard anything of me?"**

"How do you mean?"

"After the riots ended. Any news."

"Only that you'd killed yourself." I ventured a small, forced laugh. He did not reciprocate. In fact, he looked down at the table.

"That one is quite pervasive." Even with his voice disguised, he sounded quieter.

I quickly jumped to change subjects. "How long have you been out here?"

He tilted his head, still looking down. **"Here?"**

"This..." I gestured around us. "...shack."

"Ah. Around a month."

"How have you managed to live like this?"

"Offerings. Food. They leave me sustenance hidden in park trash cans."

"And how long have you been in California in general?"

He looked back up at me. **"A month longer. I heard that you were here. It simply took me a while to find you."**

I felt myself shiver. More people searching for me. "How long have you been looking?"

"I started walking west after the riots ended. That you came here as well and were on the way was simply good fortune."

"*Walking?*"

"I also hitchhiked. Begged for money on the streets. Stole food where and when I was able."

I couldn't believe it. Dead Richard, here, after all this time, only after having walked or meandered hundreds of miles. But it was pointless to think he was lying. "And you only got here a month ago."

"If you believe yourself to be the sole focus of my journey, then you are more arrogant than memory serves. I am here. You are here. This was enough for me to reach out to you."

I must have touched a nerve, but I was hugely relieved that Richard hadn't walked as far as he did just for this one conversation. "How did you find us, then? At the hospital. Were you responsible for those people attacking us?"

Richard let his arms hang at his sides and slouched a bit, like he was deflating. "Were the circumstances different, I would be offended, Fortunato. Yes, I was aware that you were being hunted. Against my will and my wishes. Pursued."

"I came to this place hoping to find respite from their ilk. The fervent and the mundane. They are restless in their devotion to something they have no knowledge of. They knew that I wished to meet with you, and some of them got it in their infected and empty minds that bringing you here by force would appease me. Grant them my favor."

"The night before their assault took place, one, smarter than the rest, sent me a message detailing their plans. They had debated. Argued. Fought over it, in their little world. I went to the hospital only because I knew that it was close to where 3:16 lived. I was lucky."

"You're not...in charge of them? Or something?"

"If you truly believe that then you do not know me as well as you thought you did."

"Sorry. More of Arthur's suspicions than mine. Where are they now?"

"You need not worry about them ever again, Fortunato. They will trouble you no more."

"I'm just supposed to take your word for it?"

"There is no greater guarantee."

"Fine. Well, I'm here. Why did you want to meet with me?"

Dead Richard shook his head. "We will get to that. First, tell me why you decided to come."

"I..." I was taken aback. "I was curious."

He just stared at me - or, at least, I felt like he did. "You were curious."

I shifted uncomfortably. "Is that not reason enough?"

"Disappointing." He crossed his legs. **"I thought you would be braver. I am fine to make polite conversation until you are ready. Who else have you met with in the city? Any other comrades?"**

I had not come all the way out here, to meet with someone clearly deranged and possibly dangerous, to be called a coward and mocked, and I felt myself getting a little frustrated over his know-it-all attitude. I liked it better when he was silent. Wanting to jab back at him, I suddenly remembered that I was not the only one getting followed against my will.

"Yeah, somebody actually came looking for you too."

He sounded unimpressed. **"You have your troubles and I have mine. That they overlap and think we know one another's movements is unsurprising."**

"This one was different, though. He said he'd been following you for a long time. And," I added, remembering, "he had a knife."

That caught his attention. He slowly straightened up. **"Ah."**

"You know who I'm talking about?" I had caught him off guard.

"The Applebarn. He's moved faster than I anticipated."

And as soon as I was triumphant, I faltered. "The...applebarn?"

"Ronin in a trucker hat. Trashbag samurai. The Applebarn. He has indeed been hunting me for longer than the others. Much longer." He began tapping his fingers on the car door, thinking.

I remembered the logo on his hat. So that's where he got the name from. Another pointless alias. "He had it in for you. Why does he hate you so much?"

He absentmindedly looked over to the hole in the ceiling behind me. He stopped tapping his fingers. "His trashbag. Do you know what else he carries in it?"

"No."

"A copy of the Bible, the Koran, and teachings from the Buddha. In his repeated readings of these, he has come to the conclusion that I am evil, and must be destroyed."

"You're serious? How do you know this?"

"Those who follow you and I have encountered him and speak of him in whispers. He wishes to avenge the ghosts of people he does not know by slaying someone he has never met. I admire him. His devotion. His dedication to his cause, despite disagreeing with it."

"Well of course you'd disagree with it, Richard. He's insane. He wants to kill you." But he shook his head.

"His idea of evil. One of my few criticisms against him."

"What?"

"There is no such thing as evil people, Fortunato. Just the broken. That he holds the idea so closely is immature."

"I…" I rubbed my eyes. These types of conversations again. I guess Dead Richard wasn't above them. "He really wants to kill you, Richard. And he's been following you forever. Aren't you worried?"

"Yes. He will kill me, one day. He has decided so."

"You act like you don't have a say. What, are you just going to let him do it?"

"At first, I was furious that this had happened. It is true. But as time has gone on, I have come to accept it."

"How did you know? Why don't you fight back?"

"You misunderstand. There is no fighting back. He has claimed my life, already. It has been decided that I will die at his hand." He spread his arms wide. They were like bird bones, a wingspan without feathers. "But I do have a say, Fortunato. I will decide where and when my life will end. He will chase me, and some day, years from now, in a place of my choosing, when I am tired of living, he will be granted his wish."

I could only try to pretend to follow his line of reasoning. "What if you die before then?"

"That is impossible. Like I said. Once a curse. Now a boon. The world is open to me like never before."

"What is *that* supposed to mean?" He waved a hand again, dismissing another thought out of the air that wasn't even worth his time.

"It is pointless to talk about the past, and its regrets, and about me. We are getting off topic. Who else have you met?"

"Richard. Answer me."

"There are contracts, Fortunato, older than the soil underneath us and bound in the space between our spirits when the will is strong enough. I have been tied up in his fate, and he in mine. He is my shadow, to be certain, but I am his light."

"But..." he trailed off. "Do not pity me. I am lucky. I have no equals on this Earth. But his hatred for me. You must have felt it. It dripped off of him and trailed behind him like a slug. It rose in a vapor from his very pores and clouded him. It is tangible. No, not an equal. No. But he is a worthy hunter, a pursuer, to be certain. To have someone who despises me so much. Without having so much as met me. I could not have asked for a finer stalker."

I stared at him. Applebarn's voice sounded off in my head like a tornado siren.

"It is more than that. Richard himself..." he trailed off. "Richard...there's something wrong with him. Something unnatural, and dangerous, and constrained to him alone."

I didn't understand any of it. How could you? It was the ramblings of a crazy person. Two crazy people, who were feeding off of one another. Was Arthur right? Was I in danger? My mouth moved without forming words, but soon my voice reappeared. "E...Elizabeth. I saw her. Once."

"Elizabeth. I remember her. How was she?"

"She's...getting married."

"Elizabeth?"

"...yeah."

"Surprising. She seemed alive. Did you meet her fiance?"

"Uh, no I didn't. No."

He was watching me. Too much silence passed. "What?"

"You slept with her." My heart jumped up to my throat.

"What?"

"Out of hatred, too. Interesting."

"You don't know what you're talking about."

"Dangerous, Fortunato. Very dangerous. You've begun lashing out, acting, without fear of consequences, because for you, there are none."

Before I could snap back at him, he interrupted me with his booming voice. **"Enough of this. Ask me about the riots. We have much to discuss and it is best that we start there."**

"What makes you think I care about that?"

"That is why you are here. You believe that I have all of the answers to the questions nobody seems to be able to answer. Ironic, as the people who bother us think the same thing incorrectly."

"I don't need to ask you anything. Arthur already told me what I needed to know."

"You wouldn't have come here if you truly believed that. What did you ask him?"

"Why I got so much attention when I did. What my purpose there was."

"And his answer?"

"They...looked up to me. Or something. They saw me as an example."

He was completely still. Outside, a gust of wind shook the tops of the trees and brought some twigs snapping and tumbling down onto the roof, landing with a muffled thud on the moss.

"That is what you believe?"

"That's what I've been told."

"Mr. 3:16 is mistaken."

"Well, by all means, tell me, then. I don't care anymore."

"I'm afraid the truth may upset you still."

"Better to say it now and get it over with if that's the case."

He watched me for a moment. Then he looked out into the hole in the ceiling again, and he stood up, pushing himself weakly on the car door.

"Come with me. Let's go for a walk. The air is clean here. Fresh."

Chapter 20

We walked together alongside the creek, over stones and through tall grass that brushed against our knees and hissed with our strides. The sun was piercing through the foliage above us and shone in yellow streaks in the water as it accompanied our footsteps, quietly observing and offering no opinions. Richard was tall, taller than I remembered. At least three or four inches taller than me. He lumbered ahead of me like some great fleshy scarecrow, and I worried that in his weak and frail state, tripping over a rock or a root might break something.

"I used to think that you were a monster." His voice sounded off through the silent woods, but it didn't ever go too far. Absorbed by the bark, before some passerby somewhere might hear it and think that some forest demon was calling out to them, his words were confined to my ears alone.

"That's pretty hypocritical, isn't it?"

"Do you think I am a monster?"

"Maybe more just disturbed. Look at the way you dress and act."

"Fair enough. But I never said or did anything to that effect, did I?"

"How do you mean?"

"You are judging me based on my appearance and how I live. But when have I ever done anything beastly?"

"Well, when have I?"

He nodded. "You haven't, that is true. You never have in your whole life. Beastly, evil or otherwise. That is what troubled me. Your actions, be they of charity and good will, or of selfishness and malice, were, and largely remain, absent, from what I can tell."

I flared up again at these uncalled for judges of character. "How can you say something like that when you haven't seen or heard from me in eight months?"

"You were that way in college. Empty, and hollow. It was what drew Elizabeth to you, and in a moment of brilliance, she saw your usefulness. At first I thought you were simply aloof. But then I began to wonder if she was right, and if there was some truth to her claims."

"I wasn't that way then. And I'm not that way now."

"Tell yourself what you will."

"Well why did you get involved, then? What made you take any interest?" I pointed at him accusingly, but he was walking ahead of me. "You weren't even a student. You slept on the streets. What could you have possibly gotten from joining up with them?"

Once again he brushed my frustration off. It was better that way. Irritating Dead Richard was likely not a good idea. **"I saw the opportunity to make an impact. To change things."**

"Then tell me what I don't know about them. Why did it happen, Richard? Tell me that. Just that. No personal introspections on me, no diatribes on my moral compass or whatever. Just why what happened, happened the way it did."

He shrugged. **"It will be boring."**

"I don't care. Just the facts."

"It started out as some small thing. The kids were mad, upset. You know how they are."

"What about?"

"Nothing specific. These things never have a singular catalyst. It might've been the weather, for all I know. It had been cold the winter before. Do you remember? They walked around blue and frozen, cracks in their skin like stained glass statues turned alive, miserable and windswept. Whatever the cause, the general sense was that they didn't like the idea that they had been forced to make a decision on what directions their lives were supposed to take."

"In what sense were they being forced to do that?"

"When you reach a certain age, you are expected to know what you want to do with your life, are you not? And if you don't, you're still expected to make a decision. The choice often comes down to being between making money or doing something that makes you happy. And even then, people and their desires shift and change, often too late after they've started the course. Being faced with this and having what they perceived as being no way out, they panicked and got angry. So they saw fit to protest their predicament."

"Where do you come in?"

"I involved myself, and tried to change their message to something more impactful. Beyond the ravings of some student upset that his artistic genius was not being recognized."

"And what led you to do that?"

"Because I could, and I thought it would have been worthwhile."

That made no sense. But if this interaction was going to go anywhere, I needed to accept that nothing Richard ever said would ever really make sense. "So what did you try to change it to?"

"It does not matter where you come from or what you try to do. In the end wherever you end up, or how well off you are, is all a matter of lottery. Everyone is equal in that their path is obscured and vast and absolutely unknowable. Life, and the experience of it, is invaluable. It is too precious to assign to roles, institutions or ideals."

"That's what you were trying to get them to change their message to? That's it?"

"That's it. I thought that I was having some success. The riots came as an unexpected surprise."

"So what happened?"

"The message…became garbled. Because of you."

He spoke as he walked over a fallen log onto the other side of the creek, arms out to balance himself. We might have been talking about something as mundane as a recent baseball game, the way he was approaching this. I could see the end of the ravine just a small ways ahead, where the water ended and turned downwards.

"Fortunato, they looked to you as the epitome of what they sought not to be. Soulless. Without purpose or morality. No goals. Ambitions. Asleep with no dreams. Elizabeth saw in you the validation of their efforts. The product of their environment that they wanted to change."

"Even now, you live like this. Even now you immure yourself and seek to live vicariously through those around you who have human emotions, instead of expressing them. You have, for some reason, condemned

yourself to die. And this, Fortunato, is why I have come to see you."

Finally, we stopped walking. At the end of the ravine, it came to a cliff overlooking the rest of the forest down and out to the beach and the sea. The creek curled and billowed silently, softly into the earth and far down the slopes and towards the highway below, where it would pass under a distant overpass and mix with the ocean. Cars drifted silently and slowly far away. The sun was still high up in the air, and the sky in the scene before us was absent of any clouds.

Richard took this vantage point in for a moment, inhaling deeply, before continuing. **"Life comes at us in waves. Some good, some bad. The future is vast and it is opaque. It is always in the back of our minds, because one day it'll all end. We just don't know when - but I do, now at least. And you try to."**

We both stared down at the water, a shimmering mirror of the clear plastic sky. Without looking at me, he spoke again. **"I do not understand your obsession with the riots. It was in the past."**

For some reason I was unable to reply. My throat was stopped up, with something.

He watched the stream trickle down and away over the grass and rocks, and then turned back to me.

"Do you know why they call you Fortunato? A new moniker. I was surprised to hear it."

I had wondered that myself, ever since Don's son had called me that. But I think I knew why. My voice gurgled out, pained and subdued. "I imagine it was because of the blog."

Dead Richard nodded, impressed. **"Very perceptive, Fortunato. Yes, that was the pen name you were given, which led so many to find you here. Another puzzle. You claim to despise your involvement with them, yet the first thing you do when you move here is take advantage of your infamy and profit off of it."**

"I needed the money."

"You pretend to be above human emotion, but you have felt hatred, have you not, Fortunato?"

"Stop calling me that. You know my name."

"I find it suiting. All of your associates have aliases. You have hated since you have lived here, haven't you?"

Elizabeth. It must've been the heat, but my head was spinning, like I was getting a fever.

"Lusted?"

Lorelei. I touched my forehead. It was cold.

"Perhaps even loved?"

I was silent. He put his gloved hands into his crusted jean pockets.

"Why isn't life the amazing adventure that we all so want it to be? Instead we become bogged down by the details and cannot find beauty and excitement anywhere.

We are born and the clock starts ticking from the day we exit the womb. We only get a set amount of time, after all. In your wake lie countless dead men and women - you, the ultimate culmination of their efforts. And yet you would envy the peace of the dead rather than the endless freedom of the living. The same freedom that I sought to instill in those rioters, who feared you so, for your distance."

"Can you really think of no instances where you suppressed yourself? That is your problem. You feel, but for some inexplicable reason, you are ashamed to. You bury yourself. To be truly alive is to give in."

"I know myself, Richard."

"Do you? Tell me of your wisdom."

"Don't mock me."

"This is not mockery, Fortunato. You fascinate me. You walk the Earth as if dead, despite it being at your fingertips. You have more license to do as you please than anyone else I have ever met, yet you live as you do. Tell me what you know that I do not."

I caught myself then. I almost burst out laughing at how ridiculous this all was. I would have been embarrassed if he and I weren't alone. Was Dead Richard always so convincing, so deft in conversation? I wouldn't have known until now. No wonder he was able to turn things sour back home. I turned away and began to walk towards the cottage.

"Each social encounter requires a monumental effort, an enormous strain on your part to appear engaged or involved, interested, doesn't it?" He called after me. I ignored him.

"You are obsessed with predictability. You want to know everything that will happen, down to a second. You want to be in control, so you cut yourself off. It is impressive. I am almost envious."

My feet stopped without me telling them to. A gust of wind had somehow broken through the treeline and shook the grass around into sounding like a million snake tongues.

"We are alike, yes. We have a unique power. I push, and the world bends. Where I apply pressure, the universe bows to my touch. But you? The world makes waves and turns, but you remain stoic. You are immobile. We are cut from the same cloth, but we are polar opposites. In your learned apathy you claim to be untouchable. And for the large part, you are right."

"Yes. A soul is a burdensome thing, isn't it, Fortunato? Far better to drift through life as you have done, without really knowing anyone or doing anything."

"I've known..." I mumbled. To myself more than to him.

"Briefly. And yet still you were detached."

"What should I be doing, then, Richard?" I snapped and whipped back around. "Let's assume you're so right. What am I doing wrong, if we're all going to end the same way anyway? You said so yourself. That's what you wanted the riots to turn into."

He was only a bit away from me, but he suddenly seemed so much taller. Behind him, the sun shot through the trees and catapulted his shadow to overtake me. His voice flew at me again, but it felt like it was coming from all sides, through the forest and even from above - dark, brooding, and inhuman.

"Have you really learned nothing? Even after all this time?" He attacked, roaring through silence. Each word flew and struck like a thunderclap.

"A man is but a slave to the eternal autumn of his own heart, and should seek to surround himself with trees and wind. The passage of time is the only master to whom he must bow, the folly of his brethren the only enemy against whom he should rally. The world shall never provide him solace, and he is cursed to seek it in solitude. He is born rotting on the inside, and the rest of his life is spent wistfully trying to reclaim the memories of a dead world. Our pasts become an illusion; our lives, a waking dream."

"The world is full of people, Fortunato, people like you and me. Each one crying out silently for something

more, for a resolution to something we ourselves cannot define. It is only when we vocalize these inner crises do we find shared camaraderie in what seems so endless an abyss."**

I had covered my ears, they were ringing so loud. For some reason he had become much louder than he had been before, like his voice disguiser had broken. I looked back up at him.

"I'm leaving. Coming here was a mistake."

I turned back around and started to make my way up the path we had come from. I heard hesitation in his voice. **"You will not see me again, I think."**

"Good," I called back. For a few more steps he was quiet. I wondered if he was following me.

Then,

"Wait."

I intentionally stopped walking this time. I looked back at him again.

He had taken off his voice changer and held the small device in his hand. His mask was still on, but his voice was his own.

It was thin, as if his vocal cords were made of straw. Weak and malnourished, like its owner. I could barely hear it, even in the silence of that place.

"Please listen to me," he whispered. My ear struggled to follow his words. "If you do not change yourself, Fortunato, you will be caught in this endless cycle of misery for the rest of your life. You and I both know the truth, but the way you have interpreted it has rendered you a prisoner. By the end of this day you will see that hiding yourself away is no sure means of controlling your own destiny."

I was speechless. What had prompted him to show a portion of himself, so heavily guarded for as long as I had known him, to me? Was what he was trying to convey to me that important - and did he really think that by doing so he was "saving" me? As I tried in vain once more to understand him in the quiet that followed, he slipped the device behind his mask.

"I hope that you don't think poorly of me, in the end." And he turned around to contemplate the water, or the sky, or whatever it was that lay ahead of him. I left him there, after trying to think of something to say. But what could I?

<u>Chapter 21</u>

It took me around an hour to get to the parking lot where Arthur lay in his car sleeping. I tapped on the window and he jolted awake with a yell, and quickly unlocked the doors.

I had barely sat down before he bombarded me with questions. "Holy fuck, how was it? Did you see him?"

I was at this point so exhausted that I could only shake my head as he peeled out.

I was obviously tired, but Arthur refused to let me rest. "Did you see him? What happened?"

"I saw him."

"How did it go, what did you talk about? Are you alright?"

"I'm...fine. I don't think I should have come here."

"What happened?"

"He's living in a shack. We talked about the riots."

"What was he like?"

"The same. He actually talked this time around."

"You'd never heard him talk before?"

"No."

"Why did he want to meet with you?"

"He said he wanted to help me."

"What does - "

"Arthur, come on. Give me a minute. Do you have any water?"

He tossed me a bottle he must've bought while I was away, and drove in silence for a few blessed moments. Only when we reached the entrance to the park did he ask me again, just as I was beginning to doze off.

"Don't you fucking pass out without telling me what went on."

"He was...he wanted to help me. He said that I was living dangerously."

"Did he sic those guys on us from the other day?"

"He claimed not to. I believe him."

He looked over at me and back to the road. "Guess I'll take your word for it. What else did he tell you?"

"Gave me his spiel on the riots. Said you were wrong about how I was involved."

"Oh yeah? What did he say?"

I ignored him. My forehead was pressed against the passenger seat window, and I could hear the road through my temple as we drove on. The coastline, farther away now, disappeared past the hills and trees into the distance as we went further inland. It was only midday, and the sky was still completely clear.

To say that I regretted meeting Dead Richard might've been a bit much. I would have been angry with myself if I had let the opportunity pass. But I didn't think it would devolve into him telling me what he thought all of my flaws were. Projection, that's what it was. Had to be. I felt bad that I had dragged Arthur all the way out here on some pretense of getting closure, when all it ended up being was just more insane ramblings and nonsense. Of course it was - Arthur tried to warn me and I went ahead anyway. Curiosity had gotten the better of me once again. At the very least, Richard had promised to keep Thomas and Jenna and all of them off of our backs from now on. I could rest easily.

And yet now a part of me felt that my time in this city needed to come to an end. In reality, this had been the case since I had returned from my little sojourn back east: That there was nothing left for me here, and that too much had happened already. Too much had changed, from Lorelei to Don's departure and everyone else's thereafter. But how could I think that?

Hadn't I worked terribly hard to get that apartment? Wasn't I comfortable now - with a job, and a place to call my own? I just wanted to be happy, but happiness as I had understood it was fleeting and rare. I tried to settle for contentment, but even that had been pulled out from under me at every turn. My mind briefly flashed back to Don. He had every reason to be happy, or so I'd thought. Was he happy now, wherever he ended up? Was that happiness worth upending the lives of his wife and kids?

No, Richard had to have been wrong. *He* was the one who played dress up and meandered around the country with no purpose. *He* was the one out living in the woods like some degenerate maniac while I had a place to live and a means of income. *He* was the one that couldn't grow up and move on. What did I really expect him to tell me? What could he possibly know about me...or how I'd been living...

The heat of the car eventually proved too much, and against Arthur's wishes I dozed off for a good portion of the ride back to Berkeley, with my thoughts still bitter and my chest still heavy. Just before I completely fell asleep, I heard Arthur, who must've been badgering me this whole time still, huff in irritation and press the radio knob. After some static, some more knob twisting and a few under-the-breath swears, a song finally came on.

When a cold chill begins to burn at your very soul
That's the sweet touch of love
When just the drop of a name begins to sting your very toe
That's the sweet touch of love

Oh yes it is

Just the thought about seeing you would blow my mind

That's the sweet touch of love

Oh yes it is

I was about to give up but you came just in time

With your sweet touch of love

Oh yes you did

You brought out the best in me

Made me leave the rest of me behind

By some great coincidence I awoke just as we were pulling into my neighborhood, on the road past the bar. As we drove along, I suddenly remembered that today was the day. Barricades blocked off a portion of both sides of the road leading up to the building, and closer to the bar there were a few trucks and machines preparing to destroy my sanctuary. A small crowd of passersby had gathered to watch.

"Stop here."

Arthur jumped. "God, I thought you were still asleep."

"Pull over. I need to get out."

"What, here?"

I looked out past him and tried to spot other patrons in the crowd who might've been in attendance, but from here I couldn't see anything.

He looked back at me and back over to the bar. He shook his head, but turned in. We parked and I walked through the crowd to get to the nearest barrier.

"What is that place, anyways?" I heard someone ask.

"I don't know. I thought it was a warehouse." Another person responded. Behind me Arthur managed to push his way through.

"You know this place?" He asked.

"It's the bar."

"*That's* the bar?" I had to admit that from here the building appeared in pretty embarrassing shape. Maybe it was the dust that the wrecking crew had begun to kick up around it or maybe I just hadn't taken a close enough look until now, but the bar looked more like an abandoned shanty than a respectable establishment. Windowless, brown with age and neglect, and alone as if ostracized by other houses or shops.

Arthur thought so too. "It looks pretty...lonely."

"I guess so. Never had too many customers outside of a few regulars."

"So they're tearing it down?"

"What the fuck, what're they doing?" I picked up the squeaky voice of Walker in the crowd. He was to my right, along with Louis and George. Walker was jumping up and down behind his large friend.

"George. What're they doing?"

"How did you not see the notices?" George replied without turning around. "They were all over the place."

"He's *tearing it down* though? What for?"

Louis spat over the barrier, as if in some spiteful protest. "Beats me. I guess Leeroy must've been losing business."

"But where are we gonna go now? What're we gonna do?" Walker was absolutely devastated. George, apparently, was not. He stretched and put his arms behind his head, casting a shadow on no less than three people behind him.

"We can finally go to that titty bar." His friend behind him let out a wail.

Louis admonished him. "Oh come on. He's kidding."

"I am definitely not."

"We can try that sports bar near Stockton. I hear they've got good wings."

George sniffed. "As long as there's no fucking poetry. I can't believe you guys made me come here as long as you did."

As they turned to depart, Louis made eye contact with me, and broke into a smile.

"Hey, I know you." The other two turned and spotted me.

"Oh yeah," George nodded once. "You're a regular."

I tried to contain my surprise that they would approach me. "I guess we all were. Not anymore, though, huh?"

"Hey Louis," Walker piped up and finally, with great effort, managed to emerge from behind George. "Hey, hey, ask him." He whispered.

"Walker, shut up."

"Come on, you might as well." Louis hesitated, but, grinning nervously, he turned back to me.

"So, uh, look. Were you...uhh..."

"Were you in the High Street Riots?" George asked loudly. Louis blushed.

"Yeah I was. I can't believe anyone still remembers that."

George's eyebrows shot up his flat, wide forehead in what must've been a rare display of confoundment. Louis' nervous smile turned into a confident laugh. "Holy shit, I thought it was you. What're you doing out here?"

"Just starting over. You know."

He looked back at the other two, then back at me. He scratched the back of his neck. "Hey, uh. You got a place to go now that the bar's coming down?"

"Honestly? No. This was my favorite spot."

"Well, we're actually gonna head to this place nearby. It's not as, you know, quiet, but you're more than welcome to join us." I was taken by total surprise and very flattered.

"Really? You're sure?"

"Yeah man, join us." Walker chimed in.

George, however, was sizing me up. "You don't look like you play any sports."

"Ignore him. Want to come? I promise we won't ask you about, you know, that stuff," he added.

"Nobody cares about that shit anymore anyways." George noted.

I considered it briefly but it wasn't a good time. "I'd really like to, but It's been a long day. I think I'll just head home after this. Next time, though. You guys know my schedule." Louis laughed and shrugged. They turned and, with George pushing ahead, they forged a visible pathway out through the crowd of people. The back of his head could be seen until they were at the very edges, and then they disappeared.

Arthur, who had been quiet this whole time, spoke up from behind me. "Friends of yours?"

"Sort of."

"Sorry?"

"Maybe, yeah. Friends."

We looked back to the bar, on the other side of the road. I spotted Leeroy coming out and locking the door behind him, and being approached by a man in a construction hat. They shared a few words, then Leeroy nodded, and walked a good distance away, to the other end of the road, at the opposite barrier. Next to him was a pickup truck and I could barely make out the sight of the jukebox, glowing in the sunlight as if it had been turned on, strapped down in the bed. For some reason I felt a sense of relief - as if he might've forgotten to get the thing out of there before the building was torn down. I couldn't forgive him for demolishing the bar over a girl, but by now I had come to understand that I was in no place to judge their mysterious and unknowable relationship, and the bar's existence as a constant reminder of Lorelei had just become too much to bear. Its eradication would ease his suffering more than it would complicate my life.

The person he had been speaking to turned and whipped his finger in the air to the others.

"Looks like they're gonna get started," Arthur ventured.

"Yeah."

Suddenly there was a commotion to our left, like a swelling of excited whispers, sighs and amused chuckles. We both glanced around and saw, through various pairs of legs, no less than eight border collie puppies tugging at their leashes of their owner. Not only were they yipping and causing a ruckus on their own, but a good amount of onlookers had swarmed over to them. I tried to look past all of the heads and hills of hair and was able to finally make out the weary, patient face of Stephen, bald head glossy with sweat and patiently nodding and accommodating the enchanted crowd. Excusing myself from Arthur once again I carefully pushed my way over towards him until he spotted me.

The very first person I met in this city, and even after all this time, he recognized me immediately. He looked a lot more tired, stressed. But his eyes were still alight, and his smile was as wide and endearing as it was when we first became acquainted. He was dressed in the same cyan blue tracksuit and pants he had worn when I first met him, and was holding onto the eight leashes with both hands, but was momentarily able to release one to shake mine. "My friend. I thought I might see you here. How have you been?"

"Oh, you know. About the same." One of his puppies perched up on my left leg and was excitedly trying to sniff my hand. "What brings you out here?"

"I was taking my dogs for a walk when I noticed the barrier. They are tearing down your home, are they?"

"I think the owner was losing money."

"That's a shame, then. Were you still going there often?"

"About every day, yeah."

"Every day." He raised his eyebrows and looked from me to the bar. "What was so special about it?"

"I...you know, it was my place. My go-to."

He shook his head without returning his gaze back to me. "There are other places out there. I'm sure you'll find one you like just as much, if not more."

We were interrupted by another bystander asking if they could pet his dogs, who were still tugging and pulling with energy.

"Full of spunk, these young pups," He re-tied his grip on the bundle of leashes. "They almost never get tired. I have to take them on walks just so they'll fall asleep when I get them home."

"How is Maxwell doing, speaking of which?" I had forgotten his old dog. I regretted asking as soon as I saw his eyes lower.

"He, ah, passed away a few months ago."

"I'm sorry to hear that. How old was he?"

"17." He proudly pulled himself back up. "He lived a good, long life, to be certain."

I glanced down at the puppies, who were now laying in the shade of the crowd or playing with each other. "Is there a Maxwell II in the crowd?"

Stephen laughed. "There's a Maxwell III around here, somewhere."

We spoke a bit more about his dogs, and his retirement and his old and unused vineyard which still plagued his estate for a while longer. He finally gathered his pups and was turning to continue his walk when I remembered something.

"Stephen."

"Hmm?"

"I think I might have an answer for you, now."

Unsurprisingly, he instantly knew what I was referring to, and looked at me expectedly, excited. People had begun to disperse around us, impatient that the demolition had not yet started.

"I think that I have...I've secretly always measured my life as a series of periods in between visiting the ocean."

He was taken aback by that. "That's it?"

"Is that not enough?"

"No no, not at all." He broke into another smile. "I'm just happy that you know."

"I just thought you'd like to hear. I'll see you around."

I nodded, and took my leave. I could feel his eyes on my back, but when I turned around, he and his horde of Maxwells were already gone. Arthur, who was leaning on the barrier with his arms crossed, was looking incredibly bored.

"Another friend?" he asked almost accusingly as I walked back up to him.

"Yeah, sorry. Haven't seen him in a while."

He eyed me up and down, suspicious. "You're more popular than I remember you being."

"I'm surprised too."

"You had enough reminiscing? I gotta drive back to the church sometime."

"Alright, alright. Thanks for stopping."

I made a move as to head to the car, but he didn't get off the barrier. "So you're gonna..." He started, then stopped, his fingers absentmindedly tapping his elbow. Then started again. "You're still gonna help me with that project, right?"

"The gazebo?" I teased. He ignored me.

"I'd like to get it done sometime next month, if you're still willing to lend a hand."

"Yeah, of course. Why even ask?"

"I dunno. We hadn't worked on it in a while, I guess."

"Yeah, man. I'll help out."

Just as he pushed himself up and we turned to walk away, the machines finally whirred to life and began moving. We both stopped and watched, wordlessly, as a pair of excavators tore in from both sides of the bar with a great splintering and cracking. Wood, rotten brick and glass shattered and fell, and jets of water sprayed both the debris and the ruined building as it was slowly, bit by bit, crash by crash, rendered into nothing but torn splinters and rubble. Some of the onlookers who had turned and walked away quickly came back to watch, and I could make out through the dust and across the lot Leeroy, watching with his arms folded and pensive, as the final bricks were ripped from their foundations and tumbled down. Still the jukebox shone next to him through the smoke and grime, glowing like some strange torch behind the rising cloud of debris.

As soon as it had started, it was over in a matter of minutes. All that was left was the sound of water spraying into the white plume of soot that had plumed out of the wreckage, and a few of the workers yelling over the lot.

Wordlessly again Arthur and I turned to leave as the dust settled and disappeared into nothingness - taking with it every whisper, every word and thought that had happened in the walls of that place - when once more commotion suddenly erupted past the blockade just as we reached the car, this time far more animated, and panicked. We glanced back out of curiosity, but only when someone screamed in genuine horror did we both run back to the barrier.

The last great tragedy of the nameless, unmarked and forgotten bar was not the disappearance of its favorite daughter Lorelei, the departure of Katie and Ben, the eviction of the porn fiend or even that George, Louis, Walker and myself were to find a new place to call home. No, as it turned out, it came in its very last moments.

Leeroy would later swear that the place had been evacuated when he locked it up. He had called upstairs and nobody answered. When the big machines came and began to tear the place down, nobody heard her scream and when the dust had settled one of the workers noticed a crumpled white leg under the wreckage and everything was immediately ground to a halt. We could see it from there. I knew who its owner was immediately.

Those who had come to watch the demolition in interest were pushed back by the crew, but Arthur, in an uncharacteristic moment, asserted some form of clerical authority and stepped up to the workers, saying that it was his duty to perform last rites. He was dressed with his collar, and in the chaos and panic of the moment, nobody questioned him. When I tried to follow him in, one agitated worker stopped me.

"Who do you know here?" He put a hand on my chest.

"Everyone. Get out of my way." Arthur and I jumped over the torn two-by-fours and stones to get to where the construction workers were huddled over the body. At the sight of a priest, they stood and made room.

The Asian girl had been upstairs. When Leeroy called for everyone to get out, that it was all over, she must not have heard him; her headphones were on or something, and now under rock and wood splinters she lay covered in dust with blood dripping out of her nose and eyes rolled up and half open. She was wearing a black leather jacket and a black tank underneath, both ripped up and covered in dust and dribbles of red.

I stared at the body until I couldn't anymore, trying to understand and piece together the significance of what had happened. In what seemed like only a minute, police and ambulance sirens echoed down the streets as the tragedy fully coalesced. Arthur was still mumbling something as he knelt over her with a rosary he must've had slipped away somewhere when the ambulances and police cars pulled in screaming nearby.

Soon Leeroy was sobbing and making a statement to a paramedic and insisting that he had swept the place. But since he didn't actually go upstairs to pull her out, he could be held entirely responsible. I hope he was. Because I was with Arthur, who by some unspoken religious right was allowed to be behind the caution tape which suddenly ensnared the scene like a spiderweb, I stayed there for half an hour. I watched the medics cover her body and eventually put it into the back of an ambulance, and driven away into obscurity for all time.

I never even knew her name. What she did. Who she was. But I wonder to this day whether or not she had really not heard Leeroy, or if she simply chose to ignore him. And, if choosing to ignore him, she knew why he was calling out to her.

The crowds dispersed. I was asked to leave so that the police could continue questioning the unapproachable, shell-shocked Leeroy and the demolition crew. I was numb until Arthur placed a hand on my shoulder and slowly brought me back from me from the void.

"Come on," he said quietly. "We should go."

"Tears," I mumbled.

"What?"

"Under her eyes. They were wet. There were tears, Arthur." He just looked at me, not comprehending. How could he understand? He'd never been inside the bar. He couldn't know.

As I followed him away, I passed near the spot where she had been uncovered and something caught the corner of my eye.

White pieces of plastic and green bits of metal were smashed and obliterated under where she had been crushed. Her laptop, cracked and split, smote to nothingness. She had held onto it even in her last moments.

All of her music. Everything, everything that she had created and made on it was completely irretrievable, destroyed. Gone.

It was all gone.

www.ingramcontent.com/pod-product-compliance
Lightning Source LLC
Chambersburg PA
CBHW072209150726
48002CB00005B/1736